CONNECTING THE DATES

Exploring the Meaning of Jewish Time

Steven Ettinger

DEVORA
PUBLISHING
JERUSALEM ◆ NEW YORK

Connecting the Dates: Exploring the Meaning of Jewish Time

Published by DEVORA PUBLISHING COMPANY

Library of Congress Cataloging-in-Publication Data
Ettinger, Steven.
Connecting The Dates: Exploring the Meaning of Jewish Time / by Rabbi Steven Ettinger
p. cm.
ISBN 1-932687-20-3 (hc : alk. paper) – ISBN 1-932687-21-1 (pbk : alk. paper)
1. Jewish Holidays and Festivals. 2. Jewish Fast Days. 3. Relationship between time and space. 4. Jewish Calendar. 5. Weekly Torah Portions. 6. Shabbat and Weekdays. I. Title.

Library of Congress Control Number: 2004112410

Cloth ISBN: 1-932687-20-3
Paper ISBN: 1-932687-21-1

Email: publisher@devorapublishing.com
Web Site: www.devorapublishing.com

Printed in Israel

Table of Contents

Introduction

• • • WHEN, NOT WHERE • • •

God is infinite and eternal. In creating the universe, He simultaneously invented space and time, neither of which mattered when there was "only" God. He introduces both of these concepts in the very first verse of the Torah (Gen. 1:1): "In the beginning [time] God created heaven and earth [place]."

Place gets most of the attention throughout the creation story. However, time plays a unique role, as God seems to create it twice. In verse 5, after separating light and dark, God called the light "day" and the darkness "night." This marks the end of the first day. In verse 17, after placing the luminaries in the sky, He declares that their function will be to "serve as signs and for festivals and for days and for years."

These verses obviously raise many questions, such as, is there a difference between the first units of time that designated day and night and the second? However, they also impart crucial information, namely, that even before man or Jew,

5

there were "signs" and "festivals." The days that we, today, celebrate as holidays or commemorate as fasts or other special times are not mere historical coincidences. They are threads that God wove into the tapestry of creation itself, from the very beginning. Man just needed context and perspective in order to appreciate or understand how each thread binds.

God, in the text of the Torah, presents time first. Similarly, time is the first commandment He gives to His people: "This month shall be for you the beginning of months" (Ex. 12:2). Based on this one verse declaration, our sages teach the laws of calculating the months and establishing dates.

Rabbi Yosef Karo (Spain and Israel, 1488–1575), in the *Shulchan Aruch*, devotes twelve chapters to the laws of establishing the months and dates. The Shulchan Aruch is a foundation text of our religion that presents all Jewish laws and customs in a comprehensive and systematic way. It is not a work of scriptural exegesis or mystical interpretation. Yet, we find an amazing observation among the laws of setting time.

> The mnemonic for fixing the days of the festivals is that *Aleph* corresponds to *Tav*, *Bet* to *Shin*, *Gimmel* to *Reish*, *Dalet* to *Kuf*, *Heh* to *Tzadi*, and *Vav* to *Peh*. This means that on the day of the week on which the first day of Pesach falls, *Tishah B'Av* will always fall [the word Tishah begins with the letter Tav]. On the day of the week on which the second day of Pesach falls, Shavuot will fall [Shavuot begins with the letter Shin]. On the day of the week on which the third day of Pesach falls, Rosh Hashanah will fall [Rosh Hashanah begins with the letter Reish].

On the day of the week on which the fourth day of Pesach falls, the reading of the Torah will be concluded [the word for reading from the Torah, *keriah*, begins with the letter Kuf], which is an indication that Simchat Torah will fall on that day. On the day of the week on which the fifth day of Pesach falls, the fast of Yom Kippur will fall [the initial letter of the word for fast, *Tzom*, is a Tzadi]. On the day of the week on which the sixth of Pesach falls, the past Purim will have fallen [Purim begins with the letter Peh] (Code of Jewish Law, 428:3).

This pattern has continued even beyond the time of the Shulchan Aruch, as the seventh, or *Zayin,* day of Pesach now has a corresponding *Ayin, Yom H'Atzma'ut,* Israel Independence Day, the fifth of *Iyar* (the word *atzma'ut* begins with an Ayin). This holiday always falls on the same day of the week as the seventh day of Pesach.

I have always interpreted this unusual section of the law — not homiletics but law — to teach that dates of the Jewish calendar, and especially the arrangement of the signs and holidays, contain far more Torah than meets the eye. One generally approaches a calendar with as much intensity and depth as one would approach a phone book — they both provide important information but do not teach. Yet, if we examine the nature of the special days and their themes, many patterns and connections emerge that can fundamentally alter how we relate to God everyday.

Contained within these days and their relationship to each other are systems for moral and ethical improvement, keys to understanding God's view of history, road maps to our national past and future, and beacons to the underlying or hidden spirituality of these times. Much of the material I present is well known and familiar. Many of the questions I pose may seem obvious. However, what I believe emerges on these pages, and what I hope to teach or highlight, is the true depth of God's time.

Future Festivals

The Four Public Fasts

• • • "You Are Here" • • •

For many, the summer is associated with road trips and vacations. The children are finished with school and the weather is nice, so families pull out the maps and plan their getaways and escapes, often choosing to travel by car. Driving on the major interstate highways is rather easy; the wide array of road signs, mile markers, and billboards makes it difficult to get lost. There are also many rest areas and welcome centers that feature maps of the road and the surrounding area. These maps share an important common feature: a big arrow outlined in a bold color like red or yellow pointing to a specified location proclaims, "You are here!" What a wonderful frame of reference. Imagine knowing exactly where you are.

It is a shame that life, in general, cannot work the same way. We might be close to great fortune or personal tragedy or perhaps at a major decisional crossroad — and yet be truly oblivious to where we are. In life, we know our beginning point of birth and, if we are wise, we have an awareness of where we have been since then. However, we cannot be certain about the next five minutes, five days, five months, or five years. We do not have that map. Most of us are HERE and do not know where HERE is!

But while we may not have road maps for life, we do have something similar, complete with guideposts and mile markers. These maps are the Torah and our calendar. Every week has a Torah portion and every day has a date. Every event in our lives can relate to relevant portions, and we seem keenly aware of certain special days and dates.

Jewish lives revolve around the Torah, and the Torah and its cycle of portions revolve throughout our year. These portions are important points of reference. They are guides to past, present, and future.

But these weekly guides tend to get overlooked as time passes, just like time itself is obscured by the mundane, the habitual, and the repetitive. Where were you two years ago when we read the portion of *Bo*? What did you do last 18 Tevet or last March 18? You probably do not recall. However, if asked where you spent Pesach three years ago, or how the food was at your nephew's Bar Mitzvah, you just might be able to figure it out. The holidays and certain special events help us to focus our lives and to figure out where we are when we forget to orient ourselves on the standard markers.

• • • CONVERGING SIGNS • • •

A number of times during the year, these two sets of guides, corresponding dates and Torah portions and special events converge. For example, we always read the Torah portion of

Bamidbar on the Shabbat before Shavuot and the portion of *Miketz* always falls on the Shabbat of Chanukah. This is not happenstance or coincidence. This is part of a plan designed by the rabbis of earlier generations to teach us important lessons about how these special days impact on our ordinary lives.

Take for example the connection between the portion of *Pinchas* and the period of our year that the Rabbis call "The Three Weeks," a time that starts with the fast day of the *Shivah Asar B'Tammuz* (Seventeenth of Tammuz) and ends after *Tishah B'Av* (Ninth of Av). We read the portion of Pinchas on the Shabbat that falls either immediately before or immediately after Shivah Asar B'Tammuz. As we examine a major theme of this portion and then reflect on the nature of the fast days, we can glimpse an amazing lesson that God is teaching us about the consequences of our actions. More importantly, God points the way, with a big red arrow, to correcting past mistakes.

The portion of *Pinchas* has the unique distinction of being read more often than any other section of the Torah because it contains a description of the daily sacrificial offering, the *Tamid*, which the High Priest brought each morning and afternoon. On holy days the Torah prescribes additional offerings (*Musaf*). In commemoration of these sacrifices, on each of these special days (except Shabbat) we read the verses describing the offering for that day directly from the Torah. Thus, we read from this portion, apart from its place in the regular reading cycle, close to forty times each year and each of these times is on a joyful day. *Pinchas* thus invokes the joy of the holidays, the celebration, the passion.

While these holidays and offerings make a grand appearance in *Pinchas*, they seem entirely out of place. The Book of

Vayikra (Leviticus) deals extensively with the rituals, sacrifices, and services of the Tabernacle and the Temple. Moreover, the portion of *Emor* (*Lev.*, Chapters 21–25) contains an extensive description of the holiday cycle. This information simply does not appear to belong here. It is almost as if it was placed here intentionally, many weeks later, to coincide with two of the saddest days of the year. Reading about these holy days during The Three Weeks, such a depressing time on the calendar, must mean something.

• • • FESTIVALS AND FASTS • • •

Before we analyze the relationship between the Fast Days and the Holidays, we need to find them – or more accurately, we need to find those days for which there is a direct biblical source (biblical here meaning stemming from any place in the entire *Tanach*). Using the description in *Emor* as a guide, we find six basic types of Jewish holy days: Shabbat, Pesach, Shavuot, Rosh Hashanah, Yom Kippur and Succot. In other words, we have the Shabbat, the two Days of Awe, and the three Pilgrimage Festivals.

In Jewish law and tradition, the community can and has been called upon to fast for a variety of reasons. There is a regimen of fasting in times of drought. The community may fast as a component of prayer or to repent in the face of a particular threat. There is also fasting by communities in commemoration of past calamities. However, these fasts are not permanent parts of the cycle of the Jewish year. There are certain fasts that are observed and commemorated each year and for which there is a biblical source.

In the book of *Zechariah,* the prophet relates: "So said

God of the hosts, the fast of the fourth and the fast of the fifth and the fast of the seventh and the fast of the tenth will be for the house of Yehudah for happiness and joy and holidays and therefore love the truth and peace" (8:19). This verse identifies four fast days — one in the fourth month (Tammuz), one in the fifth month (Av), one in the seventh month (Tishrei), and one in the tenth month (Tevet). These correspond to the Seventeenth of Tammuz (Shivah Asar B'Tammuz), the Ninth of Av (Tishah B'Av), the Third of Tishrei (the Fast of Gedaliah – *Tzom Gedaliah*), and the Tenth of Tevet (*Asarah B'Tevet*). These fast days are universally recognized as days of sadness, impending destruction, exile, and estrangement from God. Our holy days, on the other hand, represent joy, rest, unity, and closeness. We journey to the Temple to appear before God's presence, offer individual and communal sacrifices, rest, enjoy, and receive blessing and atonement. The two groups, festivals and fasts, sharply contrast with one another. Yet they converge during this time of The Three Weeks and the portion of *Pinchas*. Additionally, they seem destined to overlap, as foretold in the prophecy of Zechariah when the fast days themselves become "*moadim tovim*" (holidays). How can we understand this relationship? What is the connection between these sets of days?

• • • REPAIRING THE DAMAGE • • •

We often lose sight of the regular and ordinary — those familiar signs and mile markers that we cherish most, like our families and friends and teachers and colleagues — taking them for granted when we cloak them in familiarity and habit. Yet in the hierarchy of holy times, the day that stands at the pinnacle — the Shabbat — is also the day that is the most common, most familiar, and most automatic. There are no special calendars or calculations needed for the Shabbat to occur. Simply count six days and the seventh is Shabbat. The holiness of the day emanates from God and not the declarations of man. As we look at the holy days listed in *Emor*, Shabbat comes first, just as it was designated at the time of creation. It is the reference point for other holy days, the basis for the laws of permitted and prohibited conduct.

The *Mishnah* tells us (*Tamid* 7:4) that at the Temple the Levites would sing a special song for each day of the week. The song for the Sabbath started out with Psalm 92: "A psalm, a song for the Sabbath day." But they deviated somewhat from the words of the Psalm. The version they sang went as follows: "A psalm, a song for the Sabbath day. *A psalm, a song for the time to come, to the day that will be entirely Sabbath and contentment for the eternal life.*" In the time to come, after the *Mashiach* arrives, the world will be characterized as being entirely Shabbat. This was actually God's intention when he created man. Every day should have been Shabbat — the ultimate in holiness and in human existence. But late Friday afternoon, before the first distinct Shabbat day, man sinned. The first Shabbat became just that, a finite Shabbat, not an everlasting one. Man chose to alter the plan. His sin transformed the world from one that was "all Shabbat all the time" to one where Shabbat became something less. Part of man's ultimate goal is to restore the Shabbat to what it once was, and ultimately will be.

In a sense, because man sinned, the first Shabbat was transformed into something else, a day of atonement. The first Shabbat was a day for repentance, for accepting Divine judgment and punishment, for seeking leniency, and for *tikkun* (repair).

14

Parashat Emor uses two terms to describe the Shabbat within the same verse: "For six days you may do work and the seventh day is a day of complete rest (*Shabbat Shabbaton*), a holy convocation, you shall not do any work, it is a Sabbath (Shabbat) for God in all of your dwelling places" (Lev. 23:3). The ideal Shabbat, God's Sabbath, is termed Shabbat. Man, who must toil as a consequence of his sin, encounters the day in a diminutive, as *Shabbat Shabbaton.* Moving forward to verse 32, the Torah describes Yom Kippur as follows: "It is a day of complete rest for you (*Shabbat Shabbaton)* and you shall afflict yourselves…" This is the only other occurrence of this phrase in connection with the description of the holy days in *Emor.* What we have here is one of those big red or yellow arrows that says "Pay Attention." The Torah is establishing a connection here that may provide the key to understanding the relationship between the remaining festivals and the four fasts.

Let us look more closely at Shabbat and Yom Kippur by highlighting their differences. Shabbat is the highest level of holy day since its holiness is not dependent upon a designation or calculation. Yom Kippur, on the other hand, is dependent upon when the Jewish People fix the start of the month of Tishrei. This difference is also reflected in the punishments for intentionally violating the prohibition against creative work on these days. The punishment for violating the Shabbat is death by stoning. The punishment for a similar breach on Yom Kippur is being "cut off" by God (*kareit*). Part of the Shabbat observance is the partaking of meat, fish, bread, and wine. On Yom Kippur we are obligated to fast — no food or drink for nearly twenty-five hours.

We see that Shabbat is on a higher level and Yom Kippur

is one level down. Shabbat has the feast, Yom Kippur is the fast. If Adam had not sinned we would not need Yom Kippur. The day is designated for atonement and correction. We live a day as angels in order to return as repaired men.

God's Shabbat and man's Shabbat Shabbaton should be the same — God intended them to be the same. They will be the same in the future when every day is entirely Shabbat. However, until that time, God has given us a reminder, a day that is similar to but less than the ultimate Shabbat. This day is Yom Kippur. Yom Kippur testifies that man can diverge from God's plan. However, through repentance and atonement it also signifies that man can rebound and correct himself. Thus God establishes a relationship; the fast day represents the taint within a corresponding holy day. If man repents then joy and holiness can be restored.

We can use this relationship, as well as the *Pinchas*/The Three Weeks juxtaposition, to understand the connection between the fast days and the holidays. Each holiday represents a particular ideal — a lesson or characteristic that God hoped to infuse within us. Each fast day represents man's choice to deviate from God's plan.

• • • Rosh Hashanah And • • • Tzom Gedaliah

Rosh Hashanah contains many themes, reflected in its many names — The New Year, The Day of Judgment, the Day of The *Teruah* (Blowing), The Day of Remembrance. The liturgy of the holiday is also varied: "This is the birthday of the world; This is the day on which all living things stand before God as He judges and decides who will live or die and who will prosper or suffer;" As the shofar sounds we tremble in awe.

In actuality, all of these themes and images narrow down to one concept that we reaffirm many times throughout the day — God's Kingship (*Malchut*). God rules the world He created. God judges the world as an outgrowth of His dominion and our accountability to Him. His authority to dispense justice likewise relates to His sovereignty. The shofar sounds as a royal fanfare. He is "the Holy King," "the King over the entire World who sanctified Israel and the Day of Remembrance," as we proclaim in the blessings of the day. During each service on this day we invoke the following words:

> Our God and God of our forefathers reign over the entire universe in Your glory; be exalted over all the world in Your splendor, reveal Yourself in the majestic grandeur of Your strength over all the dwellers of Your world. Let everything that has been made know that You are its Maker, let everything that has been molded understand that You are its Molder, and let everything with life's breath in its nostrils proclaim, "The Lord God of Israel is King and His Kingship rules over everything."

Rosh Hashanah presents the ideal of universal acceptance of God's Malchut. However, this is not mankind's current perceived reality, as evidenced by the fact that we sin despite the fact that this violates the command of the King. Like Shabbat, this breach will be repaired. As the prophet Zechariah proclaimed, "God will be King over all the world — on that day God will be One and His Name will be One" (Zechariah 14:9). But until then we have a reminder, a corre-

17

sponding fast day. This day is the Third of Tishrei and is called the Fast of Gedaliah (Tzom Gedaliah).

The fast ostensibly commemorates the death of Gedaliah ben Achikam. When King Nebuchadnetzar conquered Israel and destroyed the First Temple, he exiled most of the Jewish People to Babylonia. However, he allowed a feeble and poor remnant to remain in the land. He appointed a Jew, Gedaliah ben Achikam, as the governor and the people of Israel enjoyed a period of calm after the terrible oppression. But soon another Jew, Yishmael ben Netaniah, killed Gedaliah, prompted by the king of Amon. As a result, many more Jews were slain, and any others that remained were driven into exile, ending the brief period of autonomy that the Jews had experienced in Israel.

So many "experts" view historical events as the result of political, social, and economic forces. If there is an evil regime, people can be rallied to topple it. An improper leader can be assassinated. Man's destiny is based on politics, negotiation, and conflict. This view ignores the majesty of God. The truth is that God controls all. Man's fate is in His hands alone. Yishmael ben Netaniah's actions are a metaphor for the false view. The Jews were in exile and the Temple in ruin because of their actions and God's plans. Any change or solution does not lie by plotting with one so-called king against another so-called king and assassinating a governor. This was not a time for political intrigue and machinations. The approach should have been heeding the prophets and returning to God and belief in His sovereignty. By pursuing the political rather than the spiritual, the result was death, exile, and destruction.

As we stray from the Malchut of Rosh Hashanah, we

stumble into the consequences of Tzom Gedaliah. The ideal is a festive day. The tainted one is a fast day. Only when man will once again universally recognize God's Kingship will the fast be repaired.

• • • Succot and Asarah B'tevet • • •

The next festival is Succot, which we commemorate by symbolically and actually leaving the comfort of our homes to dwell in huts for the duration of the holiday (seven days in Israel, eight in the Diaspora). The stated reason for this is "So that your generations will know that I caused the Children of Israel to dwell in huts when I took them out of the land of Egypt" (Lev. 23:43). Our sages debate the meaning of this verse: were the *succot* actual huts or do they refer to the Clouds of Glory that protected the Jews during their forty years in the desert? Either way, prior to the holiday of Succot we construct huts that fulfill the Jewish legal requirements and during the festival we eat, sleep, and spend time residing within them.

Succot falls at the completion of the summer harvest, when storehouses are full and food plentiful. It also falls on the heels of the Days of Awe, when we have cleansed ourselves of past sin. In other words, we are at a point in the calendar year that represents the height of spiritual and material accomplishment. We should be as close to God as possible. We should be thankful for what He has provided and how He has cared for us. We should feel secure under His wings, eager to carry out all of His commands.

Yet, something inside of us looks inward rather than out. A little voice says, "Look how well I ran my business this year. Look at the great decisions I made. Look at my education and experience. Look at my portfolio. Look at how seriously I took my repentance this year. Look at how much more charity I gave than the others. Look at how much better I am!" In fact, sitting in our comfortable homes, surrounded by our many possessions, seemingly well-settled, it is easy to lose sight of reality. It is exactly then that God tells us to leave — for the week of Succot our entire life is supposed to be displaced in a purposeful erosion of ego, a leveling of the playing field. The result is not expected to be discomfort, but JOY! "You shall re-joice in your festival ... and you shall be completely joyous" (Deut. 16:14, 15). This joy stems from knowing that we receive everything by God's grace. If we are prosperous, it is because He wills it; if we live an impoverished existence, this too is by His mercy and kindness. The rich and the poor alike dwell in flimsy walls covered by twigs and leaves.

However, we do not think this way. We value our homes and possessions and take pride in the accomplishments they represent. We do not live up to the ideal of the succah. We believe in the might of our own hands and the strength of our walls and fortifications.

This deficiency will also be repaired. In one of the prayers we offer on Succot, we exclaim, "May He erect for us David's fallen succah." The messianic age is thus characterized as the restoration of a succah! Until that time, however, we have a reminder that our Succot festival is not complete. This is the next fast in line — The Tenth of Tevet (*Asarah B'Tevet*).

From the time of Yehoshua's conquest, the Jewish People resided autonomously in the Land of Israel for approximately eight hundred and fifty years. As the years went by, they built a great society. Their crowning achievement was, no doubt, the city of Yerushalayim — with the First Temple built by King Shlomo and its impressive walls and fortifications. What could be more secure, more magnificent?

As the years elapsed, however, the people became more and more estranged from God. This corruption finally resulted in the loss of that false security. "In the ninth year of his reign, in the tenth month, on the tenth day of the month Nebuchadnetzar King of Babylon came, he and all his hosts, upon Yerushalayim, and he encamped upon it and built forts around it" (II Kings, 25:1). On the Tenth of Tevet the very symbol of Jewish permanence and prominence — the very walls of Yerushalayim and the location of God's house on earth — was officially besieged. Can there be a more shocking reminder of the message of the succah? Had the Jews of that era understood that the only way to avert the crisis was to correct their ways — to have faith in God, not to rely on their armies and walls — perhaps the outcome would have been different.

This fast highlights the folly of ignoring the joy of the festival. If we rely on strength or wealth or wisdom rather than on God, we can be subject to the whim and caprice of those who are stronger, richer, or smarter than we are. Repair of this breach will come only with complete trust and faith.

• • • SHAVUOT AND • • • SHIVAH ASAR B'TAMMUZ

While the Torah's description of the Festival of Shavuot seems to relate to the harvest (forty-nine days after the *Omer* waving, the time of the first fruits), we celebrate it in commemoration of a much more significant event. In our prayers we refer to it as "The Time of the Giving of the Torah." The Jewish

21

People left Egypt on the fifteenth day of the month of Nisan and forty-nine days later, on the sixth of Sivan (although there is one opinion in the Talmud that this took place on the seventh), they gathered at Mount Sinai and heard the Ten Commandments. When God gave the Torah to the Jews at Sinai He fulfilled His promise to redeem them from slavery. At that time the Jews also entered into a covenantal relationship with God. They accepted the obligations of His Torah and He accepted them as "a kingdom of priests and a holy nation."

This moment, the moment of the marriage between God and His people, was an ideal one. The Midrash relates that God healed all of the physical infirmities afflicting His people: the blind could see, the lame could walk, and the mute could now speak. Since the moment of Adam's creation, no human beings had ever achieved such a level of perfection and completion. Death and disease could no longer touch them. This was the ideal — a perfect merging of the Jewish Nation and the Torah — awaiting only entry into the Land of Israel to return the world to its intended course. Shavuot was this day. Each of us, along with the soul of every Jew throughout history, witnessed and participated.

But a funny thing happened on the way to utopia...

Although the Jews heard the Torah, in the form of the Ten Commandments, they did not receive a physical representation. Moshe, likewise, had not received all aspects of the Torah or the tools to teach it to the Jewish People. On that day, Moshe took temporary leave from the Jews to ascend Sinai, where he stayed for forty days and nights literally wrestling the Torah from the angels in Heaven. The day he returned with the famous twin tablets was the Seventeenth of Tammuz

(Shivah Asar B'Tammuz).

The Mishnah (Taanit 4:6) lists five terrible things that took place on Shivah Asar B'Tammuz. However, it is the first one mentioned — the breaking of the tablets — that makes this day so infamous. Moshe spent forty days and forty nights in the high reaches receiving the Torah. At the completion of this time, God fashioned the tablets with His own hands and gave them to Moshe. In other words, Moshe received a Torah, free of imperfection, directly from the hand of God. This Torah, this perfect Torah, was to be delivered directly to the Children of Israel.

On this same day, however, the Jews, who had miscalculated the timing of Moshe's return and thus began to panic, made an even greater mistake. They constructed and began to worship the Golden Calf. When Moshe saw this abominable sight, he "threw down the tablets from his hands and shattered them at the foot of the mountain" (Ex. 32:19). This happened on the seventeenth day of the month of Tammuz.

We know the rest of the story: Moshe went up for another forty days and nights to plead for their lives, and then another forty days and nights to receive the second tablets. However, at the end of the day things were not the same; they were tainted. God instructed Moshe to carve the new tablets himself, signifying that the status of the new tablets was lowered and God Himself would not fashion this second set. The relationship between God and the Jews was no longer as exalted. They would have to strive to return to where they had been. And, although God agreed to forgive and not to destroy the Jews, He did not quite forget. In fact, He rather ominously proclaims: "... and on the day that I make My account, I shall bring their sin into account against them" (Ex. 33:34). Rashi interprets this to mean that although God was mercifully withholding punishment for the moment, whenever the Jews would sin in the future, they would receive a measure of punishment on account of the sin of the Golden Calf.

The link between Shavuot and Shivah Asar B'Tammuz is quite direct. One day was perfection, the other destruction. The festival celebrates what was and what will be. The fast laments the tragedy of what now is. To put the pieces back together again we need to raise ourselves to the level our souls experienced at Sinai. Once again we see a fast highlighting the deficiency that our actions have brought into the festival.

• • • PESACH AND TISHAH B'AV • • •

Tradition and a simple look at a calendar teach that there is a direct link between the two remaining days — Pesach and the Ninth of Av (Tishah B'Av). Using the mnemonic A"T BA"SH (spelled with the Hebrew letters Aleph-Tav, Bet-Shin), we connect the beginning of the aleph-bet with the end to associate the individual days of Pesach with other Jewish holy dates. Whichever day of the week marks the first (Aleph) day of Pesach is the same day that Tishah B'Av (first letter of Tishah is the Tav) will fall that year. Some explain that this is why we represent the *korban chagigah* (festival offering) on the seder plate with an egg, which is often associated with Tishah B'Av, or more specifically with the mournful meal that we eat close to the onset of the fast.

Pesach is the festival of freedom. We all know the story — we recount it every year at our Pesach Seder. The Children of Israel suffered enslavement in the Egyptian exile for four hundred years (or two hundred and ten really intense ones). Then God redeemed them with a creative slew of miracles and wonders. The exodus from Egypt represents the penultimate redemption. It is the paradigm for all future redemptions. It is our national birth and the realization of our destiny. God did not only free the Jews, but He destroyed the Egyptians, the most powerful nation in the world at that time. God thus displayed His might to the Children of Israel, which should have instilled in them a sense of invincibility. If they had God on their side, they would witness the fulfillment of all promises and expectations. No one would stand before them. Certainly no one would prevent God from making good on His pledge to present them with the holy Land of Israel.

Tishah B'Av is the historical antithesis to Pesach. On the more obvious and eternal level, it is the day on which *both* holy Temples were destroyed. There is no greater tragedy, no greater sign of the experience of exile than the loss of the Temple. This destruction is the ultimate sign of God's dissatisfaction with His people. He, so to speak, no longer wishes for His Divine Presence to reside near us. We might even be deserving of complete annihilation. However, He chooses to vent His anger on stones and rock rather than on His people. With its destruction and without its anchor, we merely drift through history, longing for a return. Even in our modern day, with Yerushalayim located within a Jewish state, when we have access to the very site of the Temple, we still experience the exile, and perhaps even feel it more acutely. What frustration to be so close yet so far!

Less famously, another tragic event took place on Tishah B'Av, which according to tradition, accounts for why the day was destined for such great tragedy. Early in their second year in the desert, the Children of Israel were ready to claim the Land of Israel. They had recovered from the Golden Calf incident and received the Torah, built the Tabernacle (a portable Temple), which made God's presence visible in their camp, and raised a proper army. Then they paused to perform one more preparatory task. They sent scouts or spies to report on the land, its inhabitants, and fortifications. The spies returned with a discouraging report and the people despaired.

Although the Jews had witnessed the ten plagues, the splitting of the sea, and hundreds of other miracles, they panicked. After hearing the report of the "bad" spies, "the entire assembly rose up and gave forth their voice and the entire nation cried that night" (Num. 14:1). That night was Tishah B'Av.

As a result of that weeping, God proclaimed that since they cried on that night without cause, He would give them future cause to cry on that very date. Aside from the destruction of the Temples and the other tragedies related in the Mishnah (Taanit 4:6), the liturgy of Tishah B'Av, collected as a book of *Kinot*, relate many historical tragedies that befell Jewish communities — pogroms, massacres, inquisitions, expulsions, and holocausts — on that same date.

By believing the spies and despairing, by ignoring God's ability and commitment, they spoiled the redemption from Egypt. Pesach is festive, but we still end our seders on a pensive note — *L'shanah haba'ah b'Yerushalayim!* (Next year in Yerushalayim!) Tishah B'Av is the taint and the ultimate in tragedy and exile. The fast highlights our weakness and our obligation to correct. If you are tempted to shout "Why me? Why us? I was not there, I did not doubt, I did not destroy," just remember that our sages teach that any generation that does not bring about the redemption and the rebuilding of the Temple, and any generation that has not repaired the breach, is likewise culpable.

• • • Repayment and Reward • • •

This all seems fairly depressing. We had these wonderful holidays and a model for the ideal relationship with God and we stumbled. The public fasts are direct reminders of our deficiencies. However, there is hope. More than that, there is a promise!

Yes, the portion of Pinchas with its holiday offerings is always read when we encounter two of the worst fasts, perhaps the ones that represent the root cause of all later difficulties. However, rather than being a symbol of what was or could have been, this portion actually provides a message of hope. The time will come when the divergence between the actual and the ideal caused by man's poor choices will be corrected. At that time, the holidays will return to their intended glory. However, in fairness, God would not leave the other days, the fast days, behind. They deserve reward. They deserve elevation. This, in fact, is what they will receive.

We can see this so very clearly by returning to the very words from *Zechariah* with which we started:

> So said God of the hosts, the fast of the fourth and the fast of the fifth and the fast of the seventh and the fast of the tenth **will be for the house of Yehudah for happiness and joy and holidays** and therefore love the truth and peace.

This time we move the emphasis from the present, from the dates of the fast days, to the future. They *will* be for *happiness* and *joy* and *holidays*! When you encountered this verse the first time, you may have found it rather strange. Is it not enough that they merely fade away? Would we not be pleased if they reverted to the merely ordinary, which would signify that the taint is gone? But God does not act or think like we do. He loves "truth and peace." If these days have suffered alongside us and motivated us, in order to ultimately fulfill their mission they must be rewarded, they deserve to be elevated. May we merit to see these new holidays in our days — or even better, may our actions be the catalyst for repairing the damage of ages.

Cleaning Our Souls

The Holiday Seasons of Nisan and Tishrei

• • • IF I COULD TALK TO THE ANIMALS • • •

I remember, when I was young, reading a series of books about Dr. Dolittle, an amazing character who literally could talk to the animals. The Midrash relates that King Shlomo had the same ability and even relates a number of fanciful tales involving interactions that he had with a variety of animals and even insects. However, my recollection of Dr. Dolittle, at this moment, is not drawn from his character or exploits, but from one particular animal that was a part of his retinue. This animal was called a "pushmepullyou." It was essentially a llama that had two heads, one at each end of its body. If one head was moving forward, the other would be moving backward. Observing it, you could never quite tell if it was coming or going or which end was leading and which was following.

As we examine the two most intense holiday seasons of the Jewish calendar, the cluster of activity in Nisan and the cluster in Tishrei, we get hit with that same "pushmepullyou" feeling. In both months, Nisan and Tishrei, we make many preparations, we perform many rituals, and we relate to God in very intimate ways. What I have found over the years is that the more you reflect on these days, the more they seem to merge. God is teaching us and helping us to achieve a higher spiritual awareness by reinforcing the same lessons — with only slight variations. In a sense, these two key months represent the ultimate set of connections.

Let us start by listing the most obvious connections between the Elul/Tishrei season and the month of Nisan, as well as the period between Pesach and Shavuot in order to get a sense of how closely linked they really are:

- We identify the first day of Tishrei as Rosh Hashanah, the New Year, the day on which God created the world and on which He judges all living things. In Exodus 12:2, in the very first mitzvah given to the Children of Israel, God declares that for the Jews, the month of Nisan is the first of the year — their own Rosh Hashanah.

- There are seven days between Rosh Hashanah and Yom Kippur. There are seven weeks between the start of Pesach and the holiday of Shavuot.

- The Jews received the Torah (the Ten Commandments) in oral form on Shavuot. They received the second set of tablets, their actual receipt in permanent written form, on Yom Kippur.

- Thirty days before Rosh Hashanah we turn our focus toward *teshuvah*. In the Sephard tradition, the *Selichot* (penitent) prayers are recited each morning. In both Ashkenaz and Sephardic communities, we blow the shofar at the conclusion of services each morning as a wake up call for repentance and we add Psalm 27 to our prayers twice each day. According to *halachah* we not only begin studying the laws of Pesach thirty days before the festival, but with regard to a variety of legal rulings, we must already be concerned with the *chametz* in our possession during this thirty-day period as well.

- We identify Rosh Hashanah with God's creation of man. On Pesach, God essentially created the Jewish Nation. In truth, these two creations fit together, or perhaps more accurately, the second actually completes the first. When we recite the *kiddush* every Shabbat, the day on which we commemorate creation, we start by saying that God "gave us His holy Shabbat as a heritage, a remembrance of creation, the prologue to the holy convocation," yet we then quickly add, "a memorial of the exodus from Egypt." In fact even as we recite kiddush on Rosh Hashanah itself we still proclaim the day as "a memorial of the exodus from Egypt."

- Rosh Hashanah is a Day of Judgment. In our prayers we observe, "and all of mankind *passes* before you like members of a flock." On Pesach we find a similar passing of judgment, only this time it is God passing through Egypt and judging and punishing them during the Plague of the Firstborn, as we recite in the Haggadah, "and I *passed* through the land of Egypt that night." Moreover, according to a Midrash that Rashi cites in his comment to Exodus 13:18, God judged the Jewish People during the Plague of Darkness and He found only one fifth of the people worthy of redemption. He killed the rest and disposed of them when the Egyptians could not see.

31

- Both periods are times of cleansing. During one we clean out external chametz; during the other we concentrate on cleaning out internal sin.

- God created the world with ten utterances and He afflicted the Egyptians with ten plagues. We also recite ten verses from Tanach during each of the three special portions of the Musaf service on Rosh Hashanah (*Malchuyot, Zichronot, Shofarot*). Finally, when God gave the Torah, He initially presented it (on Shavuot and Yom Kippur) as Ten Commandments.

Now that we have established some of the connections, it will be important to look at the "pushmepullyou" aspect of these two seasons. In other words, what separates them and our experiences of them?

• • • THREES, FOURS, AND SEVENS • • •

If one had to associate a number with Pesach it would no doubt be four: we drink four cups of wine, we ask the four questions, we describe the approach for educating the four sons, and God used four distinct expressions to describe the redemption (Ex. 6:6, 7). On the other hand, if one were to choose a number for the High Holy days it would likely be three: we have the two days of Rosh Hashanah plus Yom Kippur, there are three types of shofar sound (*tekiah, shevarim, teruah*), we are instructed that three things can remove a harsh decree — repentance, prayer, and charity (*teshuvah, tefillah, tzedakah*), and there are three special portions of the Musaf service on Rosh Hashanah (*Malchuyot, Zichronot, Shofarot*).

Who knows three? Who knows four? Three are the *Avot* (our fathers, Avraham, Yitzchak, and Yaacov). Four are the

Imahot (our mothers, Sarah, Rivkah, Rachel, and Leah). In other words, three is the number that represents the masculine characteristics of our people and four is the feminine.

Applying this in an overly simplistic way, one might be tempted to think that Pesach is the women's holiday — since they assume the bulk of the responsibility for the holiday preparations: the cleaning, the baking and cooking, and managing the process of changing over the home — while the *Yamim Noraim* fall to the men — who get up extra early for selichot, sit in synagogue all day, conduct and lead the services, etc. However, this cannot be the basis for the two seasons — a time for men and one for women. Roles are not so fixed and both sexes of Jews are intimately involved with rituals and spirituality these days. But, as we move from the simple to the abstract, we discover that God is giving us an amazing opportunity to systematically improve ourselves each year. He does not expect us to get it all right at once. He breaks it up into manageable tasks and associates different holidays with different parts of our lives and aspects of our personalities.

The most obvious example of this acknowledgement of difference is the fact that God sometimes presents Himself using different names. When He is called Hashem, He expresses the characteristic of *rachamim* (mercy) and at other times He is called Elokim, representing the characteristic of *din* (strict justice). We, of course, declare each day, "Hashem Elokeinu Hashem Echad," confirming that both names and both attributes, mercy and justice, are all part of one God. God likewise requires us to reconcile different characteristics of our nature. He created man as a combination of physical (*guf*) and spiritual (*neshamah*) elements. If we had to associate each of these

33

parts with a gender, in a universal sense, we would likely associate the physical — labor, war, toughness, strength — with the masculine, and the spiritual — emotion, spirit, compassion — with the feminine. Each of us has within us elements of both physical and spiritual humanity and we each are challenged to reconcile and direct them toward service of God.

In order to manage our natures, God has given us mitzvot, the six hundred and thirteen Commandments. However, from the very beginning, when He set out the Ten Commandments, God provided a key to understanding His system. He divided these commandments into two categories: those between man and God (*bein adam laMakom*), represented by the first five on one tablet, and those between man and his fellow (*bein adam lachaveiro*), represented by the second five on the other tablet. We interact with our fellow man primarily within the physical realm. We interact with God within the spiritual realm. Unfortunately, we violate the commandments and sin in both realms. The corrective is the process of teshuvah, repentance. However, in order to repent we must change our very nature, which leads us to fall into patterns of misconduct, drawing us further and further from God. The holy days that we have been discussing actually guide us and show us how to change.

The High Holy Day period seems clearly identified as a time of spirit. We search our souls, we confess, and we pray. There are few physical demands (in fact, on Yom Kippur we separate as much as possible from our physical needs — no eating, drinking, bathing, anointing, etc.). This is the time when we seek to remove the distance between us and God. He is closer to us during this time than at any other time of the year. With relatively little effort, after only seven days perhaps,

God is willing to completely forgive all transgressions and to wipe our slates clean. The scarlet thread turns white as snow. With a mere week's preparation we can even receive the Torah on Yom Kippur!

This is at once astounding and yet understandable. Since God sets and enforces the rules, when it comes to dealing with the realm of bein adam laMakom, He can be merciful and lenient, placing our small steps in context and treating them as big ones. He does not need us to prove that we have changed — He knows what is in our hearts at the moment. He knows that in our own limited way we are sincere. He is satisfied that during an intensely "feminine" time of spirituality, mankind can reach inside and control the physicality and turn completely to God. This very ability of our nature is why the time that should be one of "four," feminine spirituality, is instead so thoroughly linked with "three!"

The process of controlling, repairing, and correcting the defects in our physical natures is not quite as easy. First of all, it generally takes another act to fix a wrong act. If you break your friend's window you have to pay for it or install another one. If you damaged someone's reputation, you need to take steps, if possible, to publically retract and to help them rebuild it. Improvement here is more than words and introspection; it is work. The work is initially symbolized by the physical effort of removing the chametz from our possession.

Pesach and the month of Nisan is like a Rosh Hashanah for confronting and improving the physical aspects of our nature. This process is more in our hands than in God's — because the physical world is one of interaction with others. It is the world of man and his fellow, bein adam lachaveiro, where the interactions are so much more complex and the changes must be directed outward.

This process revolves around the number seven. Because it is so much more involved, we require seven *weeks* rather than days to improve this conduct! When God judges us as men, the universal time is fine. When he judges us as a nation, as Jews — when He looks to judge how we treat each other — this requires a unique period, one associated with our national growth and development.

Tishrei is certainly a time of teshuvah for all sins, even those bein adam lachaveiro. We certainly do not neglect teshuvah for the physical. Likewise, in the Pesach/Shavuot season as we prepare for and reexperience "Matan Torah", the giving of the Torah at Sinai, we do not ignore the spirit and our bein adam laMakom relationship. But by paying close attention to the similarities and the differences, perhaps we can learn a lesson about method, emphasis, approach, and balance.

The bottom line is that we must be complete. We must serve God with both body and soul. Three **plus** four **equals** seven. We must use the seven days of Tishrei, together with Rosh Hashanah and Yom Kippur, as well as the seven weeks of the Omer, together with Pesach and Shavuot. God presents us with these opportunities each year. These are just the facts!

• • • THE NUMBER TEN • • •

At God's request, Moshe repeatedly warned and challenged Pharaoh with various plagues during the nearly yearlong process leading up to the redemption of the Jews from Egypt. The Jews themselves were, for the most part, passive observers. They were generally untouched and unaffected by the plagues (although according to the Midrash, many unworthy Jews died during the plague of darkness) and neither God nor Moshe made any demands of them during this time; they were neither requested to fast nor to pray nor to take any action. All of this changed immediately before the tenth and final plague, the Plague of the Firstborn, when Moshe transmitted a number of commands and instructions to the Jews.

The first of these commandments is the mitzvah to establish a calendar (there is a nice symmetry to giving an enslaved nation perhaps the greatest symbol of freedom — control over time itself). Rashi's commentary on Genesis 1:1 identifies this as the first mitzvah in the Torah: "This month, the month of Nisan, is to be for the Jewish People the first month of the year" (Ex. 12:2). For them, it replaces Tishrei as the beginning. They now have their own new beginning.

However, the first of Nisan is not given any particular significance at this time. God moves forward in the month to the tenth day to identify the next action point. "Speak to the entire assembly of Israel saying: On the tenth of this month they shall take for themselves, each man, a lamb or kid for the household (Ex. 12:3)." They would hold and watch over this lamb for four days, slaughter it on the fourteenth (and place its blood on their doorposts), and roast and eat it on the eve of the fifteenth (which we now celebrate as Pesach).

Rabbi Chaim Elazar Shapira of Munkatch (1871–1937, Hungary) focuses on this redemption process and the fact that it started on the tenth day of the month. Why the tenth and not the eighth or ninth or eleventh or twelfth? Referencing the Zohar, he explains that the Torah is creating a parallel between this tenth and another one — "But on the tenth day of this month it is the Day of Atonement" (Lev. 23:27). This tenth of Nisan for the Jewish People was not a mere packing day or a time to play with animals; it was a time for repentance — for introspection and spiritual preparation. Perhaps they were on the precipice of their physical liberation, but for the Jew, the soul must likewise be ready.

We find that the festival of Pesach, or Passover, has other names, as well. It is also called The Festival of Matzot and the Festival of Spring. There are a variety of laws and observances attached to this holiday, including: the Paschal Lamb, the seder, the four cups of wine, eating matzah (unleavened bread) and *maror* (bitter herbs). There are so many laws that we are instructed to begin reviewing the laws thirty days before the holiday.

However, as you begin to review these laws, you see that we seem mainly concerned and involved with only one law. In fact, it is the only law that, as a Torah commandment, applies throughout the entire festival. This is the obligation to rid our homes of chametz (unleaven). During the entire festival we may not eat (*achila*), enjoy (*hana'ah*), or possess (*bal yeroeh ubal yimotzeh*) chametz. In fact, if one will be traveling from home within thirty days of Pesach and does not plan to return before the end of the holiday, one is still required to search the house for chametz the night before he leaves and to nullify the chametz that he owns.

The balance or difference between dough that has become chametz and that can be used (which for simplicity's sake we will call matzah) is quite delicate. If the dough is completely baked within eighteen minutes of the water mixing with the flour, you have matzah. If the elapsed time is eighteen minutes and one second, the mixture is chametz. The difference between the two is so miniscule, and yet halachah treats this difference as a wide chasm. Within Jewish law there are many rules that apply when permitted and prohibited substances are inadvertently mixed together. If something that is dairy mixes with meat or something not kosher gets intermingled with a kosher item there are times when everything is still treated as kosher. Sometimes we rule based on a simple majority of quantity. Sometimes the rule is based on a dilution of one part to sixty. With chametz and matzah there is a no-tolerance rule: any miniscule amount (termed a "mashehu") renders the entire mixture chametz — even one trillionth of a particle! Why is this law so demanding? What are God and the rabbis teaching with this model?

R' Samson Raphael Hirsch (1808–1888, Germany) deals with the system of laws involving chametz in a philosophical manner, from a very interesting starting point. He notes that the entire experience in Egypt was the result of the "Covenant Between the Parts" that God and Avraham experienced. The operative portion of this is found in Genesis 15:13 and 14:

> And He said to Avram, "Know with certainty that your offspring shall be aliens in a land not their own, they will serve them and they will oppress them for four hundred years. But also the nation that they shall serve, I shall judge and afterwards they shall leave with great wealth."

The tough part of the covenant, verse 13, contains three components: 1) They will be aliens or strangers (*gerut*) — they will not own anything and they will not belong; 2) They will be servants and slaves (*avdut*) — they will be unable to exercise choice, they will have no independent capabilities; and 3) They will be oppressed (*inuy*) — they will be deprived of enjoying life.

R' Hirsch observes these three aspects of the exile and he comments that there are likewise three aspects of the prohibition of chametz on Pesach. First, the aspect of being an alien, of not belonging or owning anything, corresponds to the prohibition against owning or possessing chametz during Pesach (bal yeroeh ubal yimotzeh). There is, in fact, a lesson here. Even as free men, what we possess is not truly ours — it comes from God and He can take it away or cause us to remove ourselves from anything, anyone, and anywhere. Second, as slaves we could only eat what and when the masters allowed. The prohibition against eating chametz (achila), likewise shows that while we think that we are free, God actually controls our physical existence. He can tell us what and when and how to eat. Finally, while being oppressed, physical and spiritual joy was in short supply. Again, even while we are free, we must understand that God, as seen through the prohibition of enjoying chametz (hana'ah), is the one who defines and sets the parameters for permissible enjoyment.

It should be no surprise then that these same three concepts are reinforced on Yom Kippur during the culmination of our repentance process. Although we refer to them as the "five afflictions" (the five prohibited activities on Yom Kippur — no eating or drinking, no bathing, no wearing leather shoes, no cohabitation, and no application of fragrant oil), these prohibitions fit within the same three realms of God's control over our lives: limiting our clothing or our relationships, gerut, symbolizes alienation and the fact that nothing and no one is ours; no eating and drinking, avdut, reminds us that God controls the conditions of our physical reality; and the prohibition against washing or use of fragrant oils equates with no enjoyment, inuy, implying that God is the One who sets the limits.

I am drawn to Rav Hirsch's analysis since it reveals a Divine plan for our historical and annual experiences. It serves as a guide for keeping the awareness of God before us constantly. However, there is a more classic and direct approach that can be found in the works of many of the masters of the mussar (ethics) movement. They use the notion of our obligation to physically eradicate all chametz from our possession as a metaphor for eradicating the evil inclination (*yetzer harah*) from our souls. (This is actually based on a discussion in the Talmud itself, Berachot 17.)

Representative of this approach is the analysis of R' Yeruchem of Mir (1876–1936) who draws on the analogy between chametz and the yetzer harah to teach us many spiritual lessons:

- Chametz causes dough to ferment and rise without particular rhyme or reason. So too, the yetzer harah affects different men differently and can affect the same man at different rates of corruption and influence.
- When the fermentation first starts, it appears as just a few small cracks, as fragile as a cobweb or the antennae of an insect. The process has a rather loose hold on the mixture. However, it rapidly becomes a tightly woven binding. The only precaution is to safeguard the dough from even the slightest infestation of leavening. The yetzer harah works the same way. A slight, delicate crack

can quickly become escape-proof shackles. The only remedy is vigilance.

- We are instructed to carefully search all of the cracks and crevices in our homes to locate the chametz. We likewise need to search the inner recesses of our souls and to be totally honest with ourselves in order to locate and remove sin from our souls.

- When we search for chametz before Pesach, we are instructed to look by the light of a candle (*or ha'ner*). Man's soul is often referred to as a candle. We must search within ourselves using our strong inner lights.

- Because of the delicate balance between chametz and matzah, when we undertake the task of actually baking the matzot, we must exercise extreme care. We can not approach the task carelessly or lackadaisically. The word matzot has the exact same letters, in the same order, as the word mitzvot (commandments). We need to take care when we do all of the mitzvot to make sure that nothing corrupts our actions or motives.

All of these parallels seem to apply to Pesach — they relate to chametz and matzah. However, all of the advice seems to be directed not only at Pesach, a festival of physical freedom, but to Yom Kippur and the period of the Yamim Noraim (the Days of Awe). The themes of teshuvah, introspection, self-correction and battling the yetzer harah that are so much a part of Elul and Tishrei confront us six months earlier in Nisan.

Rabbi Shlomo Yosef Zevin (1890–1978) in *Moadim B'Halachah* relates the following thought from a work called *Noam Megadim*. He notes that as per the requirements of halachah, only grain of the five species that can become chametz can be validly used for the matzot that we use to fulfill the mitzvah obligation. Now, one would think that it would be preferable to produce matzot from a grain that cannot possibly become chametz. That way there would be no risk that one would inadvertently eat chametz on Pesach. However, the *Noam Megadim* explains that this is not the Torah way. This is not the way to serve God. God does not want us to seclude and isolate ourselves from the world in order to avoid sin. God does not want us to be deprived of choice. When one lives together with others, works with them, conducts business with them, and interacts with them — and still overcomes the yetzer harah, this is God's way. We are all placed in situations where we could become tainted with chametz. Yet we strive constantly to remain matzah.

Parents and Children

Rosh Hashanah

• • • WHAT IS THIS DAY ABOUT? • • •

Of all of the Jewish holidays, Rosh Hashanah is the one that I have the hardest time understanding. There are so many names, so many themes, and such a disparate range of displayed behaviors.

There is a festive aspect to Rosh Hashanah in that it is a *yom tov* (holiday) representing the new year, generating much excitement and symbolism. We dress in nice clothes, we enjoy good food, and friends exchange cards and treats — all sorts of sweet things for a sweet year. It is one of the few days when virtually every man, woman, and child in the community is in attendance in *shul*, which provides a social energy, as well. But, it does not have the party horns and champagne associated with the secular celebration on January 1. There is a difference between joy and merriment.

Rosh Hashanah is also called *Yom Hadin*, the Day of Judgment. Together with the entire world, we pass before God "like members of the flock." Yet, our demeanor is not that of the accused. We do not prepare arguments, state our cases, passionately plea with our lives in the balance. Rather, many people merely zip through a few hundred pages of text, reading some words, singing others, and listening to even more, as well as a few well prepared speeches. It almost sounds more like a political convention than a gathering that determines our fate for the upcoming year.

The Torah calls this day *Yom Teruah* (The Day of the Shofar Blast). The sound of the shofar recalls powerful imagery: the spectacle at Mount Sinai, the fury of Yehoshua's battle at Yericho, and our longing for the shofar that will herald the coming of *Mashiach*. The shofar also recalls the image of the smiling faces of children that gather around the *bimah* and look at the shofar blower (some of them holding their hands tightly over their ears) and their frowns and snickers if he does not produce the required sounds on demand.

In many of the prayers, especially in the ones that identify the day like *Ya'aleh Ve'yavo* in both the *Amidah* and in the *Birkat Hamazon* (Grace after Meals), and the specific blessing for sanctifying the holiday ("...King over all the world, Who sanctifies Israel and the Day of Remembrance"), we refer to this day as *Yom Hazikaron* (The Day of Remembrance). What is it specifically that we remember about last year? How much do we know about our heritage and history when we call upon the collective memory of the body of the Jewish Nation?

Well, so far we have four names and associated themes. The most crucial of the prayer services on Rosh Hashanah mentions and details three themes: the Kingship of God (Malchuyot), remembrance (Zichronot), and the Shofar blasts

(Shofarot). Discounting the two that overlap, we now have five significant themes that are presented to us obviously and directly. So which is the main theme?

What is Rosh Hashanah all about? It may well be that God, as well as the sages who described and arranged the prayers and rituals of this day, wanted us to be more contemplative — to look beyond the obvious so that we could discover what is really most important... and obvious!

While Rosh Hashanah fits within a number of frameworks — its relationship to the Fast of Gedaliah, the parallel with *Rosh Chodesh* Nisan and Pesach, its inclusion in the cycle of holidays, and its message within the scheme of spiritual development — it calls out for its own scheme of connection. How do all of the themes of Rosh Hashanah fit together? Does a single picture or message emerge that can teach or guide us? After all, Rosh Hashanah is the first, the beginning. It is a day that signifies the template for God's relationship with man.

• • • WHY DO WE GATHER? • • •

We live at a time where only a small minority of Jews (certainly less than twenty percent) scrupulously observes the traditions of the faith. Synagogue attendance for the majority of Jews has dwindled from twice daily to each Shabbat to major holidays, and has finally settled on twice a year — Rosh Hashanah and Yom Kippur. Before turning inward to the themes and texts of Rosh Hashanah in order to find the message of the day, it is important to reflect on what it is about this holiday that maintains the interest of an otherwise uninvolved population of non-observant Jews.

Some attend services for emotional reasons — out of

love/respect for their parents or for their children. Some people feel a need to maintain tradition on some level while others want to make sure their children have a chance to connect with God, even if they themselves no longer feel the connection. Others return each year because they understand what it means to be Jewish; they accept that they have obligations and a relationship with God. They may even have their own deals or covenants with God. But these motivating factors are not enough.

The Torah tells us so very little about this day. The only information it imparts is the when (first day of the seventh month), a name (Yom Teruah), and the offerings sacrificed. My search for answers, therefore, centered on the prayers and language of the day — assembled in the traditional book of prayers for Rosh Hashanah, the *machzor*.

• • • EVIDENCE AND CLUES • • •

The first set of clues emerges from the Torah readings and *haftarot* for the two days of Rosh Hashanah. Although there are connections between our weekly Torah portions and certain weeks of the year, for the most part we are just cycling through. We start the yearly cycle literally "in the beginning" and we divide the Torah into weekly portions until we reach the Torah's concluding words. Portions are not selected; they just occur. Likewise, the Rabbis selected text from the works of the Prophets to be read each week on the basis of their relationship to what was determined to be the theme of the weekly portion. This began during the reign of King Antiochus, when the Syrian Greeks outlawed public reading of the Torah under threat of death. To safeguard the community, both physically and spiritually, the rabbis established the reading of haftarot as a substitute until the ban was lifted. After the public Torah reading was reinstituted, the people retained the custom.

The holidays are different in that the sages had a nearly blank slate with which to work. They could select from any portion in the Torah. Of course, they wanted to establish readings that captured the themes of the day or that taught the laws and rituals of the holiday. Thus, by observing the selections, we can discern what they thought were the dominant themes of the holiday. The selection of public Torah reading for the holidays predates most, if not all, of the liturgical selections in the machzor. Thus, these themes may well have set the tone for the prayer formulas and structures that followed.

The Torah reading and the haftarah for the first day of Rosh Hashanah reflect identical themes. The reading of the entire twenty-first chapter of Genesis opens with the moving words "*VaHashem* pakad *et Sarah.*" God *remembered* the ninety-year-old Sarah and the promise that He made to her through the angels a year earlier. She would bear a son whom she would name Yitzchak. The sages teach that God remembered her on Rosh Hashanah. The reading from the first two chapters of I Shmuel relates a similar story of another righteous yet barren woman, Channah, who prays to God for a son. We read: "*Vayizkereha* Hashem," "and God *remembered* her" (I Sam. 1:19).

The connection seems obvious, but the fact is that there is much more to these readings than mere remembrance by God. While the selection from Genesis opens with God remembering Sarah, it continues with Yitzchak's birth and with the significant issues of child rearing that his parents face as he grows. Yitzchak has an older half-brother, Yishmael, the son of Hagar. He is a lively boy who seems more interested in partying than in his studies. Sarah witnesses the corrupting effect that Yishmael's influence has on Yitzchak and intervenes with Avraham to have him, together with his mother, exiled from the household. Avraham consents to Sarah's request only after God confirms the soundness of her advice. In other words, this is a terribly difficult decision for Avraham to make. Nevertheless, from a parenting standpoint, it is vital for Yitzchak's development.

As Yishmael and Hagar wander in the desert wilderness, they face a crisis: they run out of water and are at risk of perishing. In the opening portion of the narrative, we find God responding to a mother's prayer, which leads to the birth of a child. Here, the other mother despairs and leaves the child some distance away from her so that she will not have to witness his death. The child, however, calls out to God, "And God heard the cry of the child...and he [the angel] said to her, 'What troubles you Hagar? Fear not for God has heard the cry of the child in his present state.'" The prayers of the child reach to the heavens to protect and safeguard the parent!

The narrative then detours into regional politics. A local king, Avimelech, King of the Philistines, recognizes that God is with Avraham and has made him prosper. Avimelech is apparently concerned that such success and prosperity may well lead to expansionist notions. The Philistines valued their separate state and did not wish to be occupied by aggressors. They therefore proposed a plan for peace, to secure the legitimacy of their status in the region. This was a significant negotiation that many commentators describe as a serious miscalculation on Avraham's part. He should not have relied on treaties. Rather, he should have relied solely on God's promise. God made specific promises to Avraham concerning the inheritance of the Land of Israel by his children. He should not have entered into an agreement dealing with Avimelech, his son, and his grandson.

Avimelech was not proposing a short-term agreement. He wanted to bind children and grandchildren, as well. No doubt, this is why God's command for Avraham to offer Yitzchak as a sacrifice follows immediately. God is sending Avraham a message: do not take God out of your parenting equation. Do not negotiate a future for your children in a vacuum. I have set out a future; we are all in it together. We can appreciate Avimelech's concern for his children and their future. However, Avraham was aware that he was a part of a different course and destiny. He was not just a parent, but a Jewish parent — a partner with God.

Thus, on day one we have a reading with three stories. Each story is a variation on the same theme — that God takes His role as part of the parent-child relationship, or I should say the parent-child-God relationship, quite directly and seriously.

This message is reinforced in the haftarah reading for the first day. The narrative relates far more than the birth of Shmuel the Prophet after God accepts the persistent and somewhat dramatic prayers of his mother. We have a righteous mother and a pious father, who emotionally have endured much before their son is born. However, in order to fulfill a bargain they made with God, they then must make a difficult parenting decision. Their decision involves how best to put

God into their son's life — which they make by literally giving him to God. After Shmuel is weaned, his mother and father return to the Tabernacle and convince Eli the High Priest to impress him into full time service of God. The course of both the birth and life of Shmuel are determined by the parent-God partnership.

The Torah reading for day two is the ultimate parenting story, the *Akeidat Yitzchak*, the Binding of Yitzchak, which represents the ultimate challenge to the parent-child-God relationship. God puts His word and His promises to Avraham to the test by seeming to take back the one gift that Avraham treasured most — the son who represents a continuation of his philosophy and life's work.

Avraham, who has struggled throughout his life to balance family and religious obligations — first in leaving his own family in Charan, then in dealing with Hagar and Yishmael, and most recently in negotiating with Avimelech — has his core beliefs and emotions at stake. This test is designed to make him choose once and for all. Does he wish to be God's prophet or does he want to be a father? Will he love God or his own son more? As the challenge is presented, the two roles cannot be reconciled.

Finally, there is Yitzchak. He is not a mere child. He is a thirty-seven-year-old man. When he departs for the trip, he may not be aware of the unfolding drama. However, as he and his father approach the mountain without any animals for an offering, and most certainly by the time he is bound to the altar, Yitzchak himself is likewise put to the test. Is he devoted enough to his own father and does he have sufficient faith in God to suppress his own survival instincts and to allow himself to be sacrificed?

In the end, there is of course no conflict. All tests are passed and an eternal bond is forged. God does not interfere with the role of the parent. He is a full partner, a stakeholder.

The haftarah that we read on day two, from Chapter 31 of Jeremiah, is more a prophecy than a narrative. It contains many themes relating to the future redemption. However, it also contains the following interesting verses:

> So said God: A voice is heard on high, wailing, bitter weeping, Rachel weeps for her children; she refuses to be consoled for her children, for they are gone. So said God: Restrain your voice from weeping and your eyes from tears; for there is reward for your accomplishment — the words of God — and they shall return from the enemy's land. There is hope for you ultimately — the words of God — and your children shall return to their border (Jer. 31:14–16).

Rashi relates a *Midrash Aggadah* that fills in the background information on these verses.

> The Fathers and Mothers attempted to console God after Menashe placed an idol in the Temple. However, he refused to be consoled. Then Rachel approached and said: Master of the Universe, whose mercy is the most abundant — Yours or man's? Certainly Yours is! Behold how I brought my rival [her sister Leah] into my house. Did not Yaacov work for my father in order to earn the right to marry me? However, when I arrived at the mari-

tal canopy, they substituted my sister. Not only was I complicit in my silence, I even gave her the secret signs [that Rachel and Yaacov devised to thwart any trickery by Lavan], so You, God [should show equal forbearance]. Your children have brought a rival into Your house. You should stay silent [rather than destroying them]. God replied [to Rachel]: You have presented a convincing defense. You will be rewarded for your work and righteousness for providing your sister with the signs.

The haftarah is thus, once again, highlighting the operation of this three-sided relationship. In this instance, the parent, Rachel, intervenes with God to save her children.

We find the second set of clues in the Torah itself. As we discovered, Rosh Hashanah has many names and identities. The Torah itself never uses the name "Rosh Hashanah." In the only two direct references to the holiday we find two similar but different names. In Leviticus 23:24, we read: "...in the seventh month on the first of the month, there shall be a rest day for you, a remembrance with shofar blasts (*Zichron Teruah*), a holy convocation." Numbers 29:1 states: "In the seventh month on the first day of the month, there shall be a holy convocation for you...it shall be a day of shofar-sounding (*Yom Teruah*) for you." Thus, as per the Torah, this holiday is known either as Yom Teruah or Zichron Teruah — a day that relates somehow to the sounding of the shofar.

The shofar holds a direct connection to the story of the akeidah. The ram that Avraham sacrificed was a substitute for Yitzchak and thus, by blowing the shofar, (the horn from this animal) we remind God of the tremendous faith both Avraham and Yitzchak exhibited, and we invoke their merit. But the question remains: why do we emphasize the teruah blast rather than simply calling the day Yom Ha'Shofar? After all, there are two other equally important sounds — the *tekiah* and the *shevarim*.

What is a teruah? The Mishnah in Rosh Hashanah (4:9) explains: "The length of a tekiah is like three teruot and the length of a teruah is like three whimpers (*yevavot*)." The Talmud, *Rosh Hashanah* 33b, provides a little more background about these whimpers:

> For it is written, 'a day of shofar sounding (teruah) it shall be for you.' And the *Targum* [Aramaic translation, itself based in tradition] renders this: 'a day of *yevava* sounding it shall be for you.' And it is written in connection with the mother of Sisera [a Canaanite general who slaughtered and plundered many Jews in the era of the early prophets. His army was defeated by Barak with the assistance of the prophetess Devorah. Sisera himself experienced a gruesome death at the hands of a clever woman named Yael who drove a tent stake through his head after plying him with milk.]: "Through the window she looked and she cried (*vateyabev*), Sisera's mother" (Judges 5:28).

Thus we see that our understanding of the teruah sound comes from the tears shed by a mother for her son. There is a deep lesson here. The woman who was crying was a woman who routinely celebrated and encouraged her son's acts of plunder and slaughter. As Sisera left for work that morning, intent on wiping out the army of Israel, his mother, no doubt, kissed him on his cheek, handed him a lunch bag, and prayed for his success. In fact, *Tosafot*, on this same folio, tells us that we derive another important custom relating to the shofar blowing from Sisera's mother. We blow one hundred blasts because she let out one hundred and one sobs when she heard of her son's demise. The description of her reaction is quite telling. She stood by the window (or according to the Malbim she looked into her crystal ball), and when her son failed to appear on time she simply thought: "They must be dividing spoils and ravishing the women." Unlike a righteous woman who would seek consolation or hope from God or from the merit of her children, this evil woman was initially drawing comfort from what she hoped was Jewish misfortune. The first hundred sobs emerged from the vileness of her spirit. We counteract them with one hundred blasts of the shofar. However, we do not try to cancel out the last cry. Her cry of anguish over the loss of her son — a mother's honest and true compassion for a child, even a child like Sisera— is part of the theme of the day.

As we methodically and fervently read the words in the machzor, words that great sages composed to enable us to accomplish our spiritual tasks and objectives for this day, we encounter more evidence of the true theme of Rosh Hashanah:

- During the repetition of the *Musaf amidah*, after each set of shofar blasts, we recite a short passage, "*Hayom harat olam* (Today is the birthday of the world)..." The word used for birthday, harat, is derived from a verb that relates to birth, but even more to conception. Thus, it immediately introduces the parenting theme. However, the text then expresses the notion that while we approach God as servants, we also approach as His children. We ask that God accept us as children, and "be merciful to us as the mercy of a father to a son."

- In the amidah for the entire period of the Ten Days of Repentance we insert additions to the two opening and the two concluding blessings, which are common to all services. The first of the blessings of the amidah is *avot* (fathers or patriarchs), which invokes the merit of our forefathers. The addition for this blessing, "Remember us for life, o' King Who desires life, and inscribe us in the Book of Life, for Your Sake, o' Living God," introduces the themes of remembrance, the majesty of God, and our request for life in the upcoming year. It would not be necessary to reinforce the parenting theme, since that is the subject of the blessing itself.

  The second blessing is entitled *Gevurot Hashem*, God's Might, and it discusses aspects of Gods power over life and death. The addition here is: "Who is like You Merciful Father, Who recalls His creatures mercifully for life." This phrase introduces a theme that is not otherwise connected to the blessing — God as father, God as merciful parent.

- Throughout the machzor, as well as in the *Selichot* (various prayers of supplication recited from before Rosh Hashanah until Yom Kippur), we find other numerous references to parents and parenting with calls for parental mercy, parental compassion, and parental honor.

  Finally, we encounter the last piece of this puzzle. The

center of our prayer services is the amidah, often called the *Shemoneh Esrei* (Eighteen Benedictions) since the weekday version originally consisted of eighteen blessings (now nineteen). On Shabbat and the festivals, this number is reduced to seven. However, there is one notable exception. In the *Musaf* service for Rosh Hashanah, the amidah has an unusual number, with three middle sections of blessing (Malchuyot, Zichronot, and Shofarot) rather than just one. This makes a total of nine blessings — nine, as in the number of months from conception to birth. By now, there can be little doubt as to the dominant focus of the holiday. It is a day saturated with parenthood.

• • • WHAT DOES IT ALL MEAN? • • •

Trying to comprehend our relationship with God along the lines of the parent/child relationship is certainly the closest thing possible to the lowest common denominator. Is there a more universal set of experiences and emotions? Everyone, regardless of race, color, creed, or nationality is either a parent or child, or both.

The key to fulfilling our obligations to God is linked to our obligations as parents and members of families. If we are not the type of parents that we should be, if we are not the type of children that we should be, if we have not made the sanctity of our families our top priority, then we are failing them and ourselves!

The Talmud, *Rosh Hashanah* 17b, tells us about a promise that God made to the Children of Israel regarding forgiveness. After the Jews sinned by worshipping the Golden Calf and Moshe successfully pleaded on their behalf, God shared a secret:

God draped a *tallit* (prayer shawl) around Himself like the leader of the prayer service and He showed Moshe an order of prayer. He said to him, 'Any time Israel sins they shall do/make (*ya'asu*) before Me like this order [the Thirteen Divine Attributes of Mercy] and I will forgive them.'

Notice that God does not instruct that they *say* or *pray* this formula. They are to *do* — to *live* the attributes of God — to be kind, to be merciful, and to be slow to anger. Within the context of what we have discovered about Rosh Hashanah, this would absolutely include being the kind of parent that you expect God to be.

There is a story told about the Klausenberger Rav, Rabbi Yekutiel Yehudah Halberstam, and his experience in a DP camp in 1946. He was sitting in his apartment on the eve of Rosh Hashanah, preparing for what he expected to be his first normal celebration in years — at least as normal as it could be for a man who suffered through the Holocaust and lost his wife and eleven children. Suddenly, his prayers and preparations were interrupted by a small knock on the door. A young girl who had lost both her parents asked him for a blessing. He placed a kerchief on her head, placed his hands over that, and blessed her.

Minutes later, there was another knock and another girl. Then another and another and another — seventy in all! As he headed to the makeshift synagogue for services in the late afternoon he said that this experience as a substitute father elevated his Rosh Hashanah thoughts and prayers to heights he never before thought possible.

As we sit before the heavenly court on Rosh Hashanah, the numbers of billable hours that we chalked up are not important; neither are the hours spent pursuing recreation and community and organizational politics. We can truly celebrate on Rosh Hashanah if we send the message, "You — my children, my family — are the most important parts of my life, my highest priorities." God is our partner in this endeavor, and He does not like to see us slacking off!

• • • ROSH HASHANAH AND 9/11 • • •

We have now established the connections between our family lives and the holiday of the Jewish New Year. In order to take this comparison from the symbolic into the practical, I'd like to talk about a very real example of the connection. In 2001, words of the Rosh Hashanah machzor had never seemed more appropriate to me. A mere week and a few days after the terrible tragedy of September 11, the lines *"Who will live and who will die, and who will die at his predestined time and who before his time ..."* were somehow more real than ever.

When the terrorists acted on September 11, 2001, leaving horror, insanity, and irrationality in their wake, the shofar blasts of Rosh Hashanah took on a different image entirely for me. Suddenly, tekiah meant the BOOM of jets crashing into the World Trade Center and the Pentagon. Shevarim was the wail of the sirens of emergency and rescue vehicles. Teruah were the tears of victims, families, a country, a world. The nature of our world suddenly changed. Security, safety, and smugness were stripped from us in a way that made us realize just how helpless and naïve we really are. In particular, for those of us living in America, our perspective on the events in

Israel, the constant attacks on beautiful, wonderful teachers, children, mothers, and yeshiva students became far less abstract. The Israelis were sending army rescue crews to New York to help recover the thousands of dead, including many of our Jewish brothers and sisters. These things not only happened "there"; they were happening "here" as well. Unfortunately, the enormous tragedy of the attack on the World Trade Center provided an unforgettable opportunity to unite as an international family.

I would like to share some of the experiences that touched me directly that week. I am sure that these are not special or unique — but they are mine. They helped me to sort out what happened and to focus and to prepare for the Yom Tov and for the role that God plays in our lives more directly and starkly than anything else previously within my scope of experience. They certainly illustrated for me the themes of Yom Hadin, the Day of Judgment, better than any Midrash or parable that I could otherwise read or recall. These experiences will always connect and link Rosh Hashanah and 9/11 together for me.

On Sunday, September 9, I was visiting a relative in New Jersey who is a construction engineer. He was excited about the new job he was to be starting in two weeks. He was to become the facilities manager at the World Trade Center! Ordinarily, how important are any given two weeks in our lives?

On Monday, September 10, I was representing a family member on a business matter in court in the Bronx. The comptroller of the business is an old family friend I'll call Rachel. Rachel's son is a year younger than my oldest son, who was then a senior in high school. After we exchanged greetings and pleasantries, she asked me whether we were planning to send our son to Israel next year. I replied that we were. She expressed nervousness about her own decision — and I made some inane comment that sounded something like, "Are we any safer here in New York than in Yerushalayim?" Later that day, less than twelve hours before the hijackings, I flew out of Newark airport. The next morning, safely back at my desk in Detroit, part of me wanted my words to Rachel back.

On the morning of the attack several mundane changes in schedule turned into life-saving alterations. My cousin, who works at 5 World Trade Center just happened to take the day off to take his daughter to the doctor. My brother-in-law, who works for Morgan Stanley (which leased thirty floors in the World Trade Center), was at a meeting in the midtown, rather than downtown, office. My brother's son-in-law had returned home because he forgot his office keys and therefore was still on the way into work at the World Trade Center. The son of my daughter's teacher, who is an attorney in New York in the Wall Street area, missed the attack since he, like many other observant Jews that day, planned to arrive at the office a little later because of the Selichot prayers that added to the length of the morning service. Finally, a good friend of mine was commuting to work downtown on the bus from Monsey, which broke down that morning on the way in — the first time in years that had happened — making him thankfully late.

There are many more such stories — each of you likely knows of some. In fact, since then, whole books have been written filled with stories that offer a spiritual or religious perspective on that day. But the purpose of revisiting 9/11 is not to provide a platform for more "Twilight Zone" tales, as motivational as they may be. The purpose is to provide the framework for linking 9/11 with the day on which we proclaim the malchut of God over the entire world, a world that we now know is far more complex than any of us can comprehend. Using insight gathered from our Jewish sages we can approach this understanding by narrowing our focus and by examining the two most central actors in this human drama: the victims and the perpetrators.

Each day in our synagogue, I sit directly in front of Henry, a Holocaust survivor who devotes countless hours to speaking about his experiences and educating many schoolchildren about the *Shoah*. His life is dominated by that devastating experience. On Wednesday morning, September 12, he arrived at shul early and was sitting in his place shaking his head. When I greeted him, he said to me, "Unfortunately this generation will now learn what it is like to lose a loved one, so many loved ones, without a trace, without a body to bury and mourn, without really knowing why."

His words not only amplified my own unease over the World Trade Center tragedy, but they caused me to question that most unsettling aspect of the Holocaust: even if we accept as part of God's sovereignty His right to subject our people, His people, to such a severe ordeal, why were so many cremated or lost in unnatural ways, especially in light of the sanctity of the body and the importance of Jewish burial practice?

Later that week, as I prepared for my weekly Midrash class, I came across an astounding insight which, for me, provided an acceptable or understandable answer. This Midrash, in the portion of *Vayelech* (read either on the Shabbat immediately before or immediately after Rosh Hashanah), provides a discussion of the events surrounding the death of Moshe:

[After a person dies], all people [the word used is *briyot*, all people, not just Jews] are involved with funeral implements that are man-made — the casket, the shrouds, the funerary bed, but You [God for Moshe] prepared heavenly implements, heavenly shrouds, a heavenly casket, a heavenly funerary bed. Another explanation: When an ordinary person dies, he is attended to by his relatives and neighbors, but you [Moshe], I [God] and the heavenly assemblage of angels will attend to you (*Devarim Rabbah* 9:5).

This is the true fate of the *kedoshim* (holy ones), both of the Shoah and those that perished at the World Trade Center or in terrorist bombings and whose bodies will never be recovered. God, our King, the King of the World, The King of all Mankind, personally attends to them with love, respect, truth, justice, mercy, and understanding. Our responsibility on Rosh Hashanah is to appreciate and acknowledge Him and how He undertakes His role. It is easy to admire the King who provides everything good. We must admire the King who provides everything, and from whom everything ultimately is good — even when we do not or cannot understand.

It is easy to understand the victims, to place them in a spiritual light, to give their deaths meaning, and to push away the negative. But how do we understand the perpetrators, the raw evil that they represent? They seem to be the antithesis of the *middot* (characteristics) of God.

I do not know or understand the psychology of such evil and suspect that no insight can do anything for those who have perished as a result of its handiwork. But I am aware of a story related in the Talmud (*Avodah Zarah* 17b and 18a), referenced on Yom Kippur, which provides its own message of hope for such people, despite their evil actions. The story is as follows:

> Rabbi Chananiah (Chanina) ben Taradyon was one of the famous Ten Martyrs. When the Romans came to kill him, he was teaching Torah, surrounded by his students and carrying a Torah scroll in his arms. The Romans unrolled the scroll, wrapped him in it, tied him with a bundle of twigs, and prepared to set him on fire. Before they lit the flame, they soaked strips of cotton wool in water and placed them upon his heart to prolong the suffering. They then lit the fire.
>
> As the flames began to consume the twigs and the parchment surrounding his body, Rabbi Chananiah gazed upwards oblivious to the flames. "Rebbi, what do you see?" asked his students — for he seemed engrossed in a wondrous sight. "I see parchment burning and letters flying into the air," he answered. "Open your mouth and let the fire inside, so that you will not suffer long," they pleaded. Rabbi Chananiah refused. "It is better that He Who gave me life should take it from me. I will do nothing to hasten my end."
>
> The executioner witnessed this exchange. "Rabbi," he asked, "if I make the flames hotter and I take

the wet wool off of your chest, will you bring me to *Olam Habbah* (the World to Come)?" "Yes," said Rabbi Chananiah. "Swear it to me," the executioner demanded. Rabbi Chananiah swore. The executioner fanned the flames, ripped the wet wool from his chest, and the *tzaddik's* holy neshamah flew to the heavens.

Grasping the moment, the executioner leapt into the flames. Immediately a *Bat Kol* (Heavenly Voice) announced, "Rabbi Chananiah ben Taradyon and the executioner were ready to enter *Olam Habbah.*" Rebbi (Rabbi Yehuda the Prince) heard this and cried. He said, "One earns the World to Come in a moment and another earns the World to Come in a lifetime."

How did this happen? How did the executioner change and how did he merit such a great spiritual reward, a portion in heaven, in a mere moment?

The executioner was a ruthless, vile, cruel, evil man. He spent his life killing and torturing people — most of them likely Jewish. But he had never encountered a righteous man, a tzaddik like Rabbi Chananiah ben Taradyon, before. Rabbi Chananiah's behavior transported him — he somehow understood that the man he was trying to kill was more an angel than a human. He saw the way the rabbi bore his suffering. He witnessed the exchange between the tzaddik and his students. He heard the description of the letters of the Torah flying to the heavens. At some point a powerful message reached this savage: *This rabbi is not your victim, he is the victor, the conqueror!*

Rabbi Chananiah, who displayed such an intense attachment to his Creator, was going to a world of purity and holiness. At that moment, the evil executioner lost all interest in this world. He wanted a piece of the holiness that he witnessed. This world and what he thought were its priorities and rewards suddenly lost their appeal. The executioner perceived the ultimate truth — Reality, with a capital R.

We can all only hope that those who seek to corrupt God's world, who bring chaos and death, who cause innocent people to suffer and who take passions and fervor and distort them into evil, all experience this epiphany — so that they and the rest of the world can proclaim, "*Hashem Elokei Yisrael Melech u'Malchuto bakol m'shala*" (The Lord, the God of Israel is King and His Majesty extends over all).

We are not victims and should not act like we are. We certainly are not corruptors and evil perpetrators. All we can do is to be God's loyal subjects by setting the example and spreading the values of His Torah. The two towers fell, but the two tablets still guide us to all corrections and solutions. Is it not interesting that ten falls between nine and eleven? Take out the ten and it all falls down!

Touchdown and the Extra Point

Succot

• • • KEEPING SCORE • • •

The world of sports has, in a sense, evolved into its own religion. Each individual sport has rules, regulations, and interpretations — its own bible, so to speak. Sports have myths and legends. There is an almost cult-like devotion that people display in connection with their home teams. Fans can go to extremes in their "worship" of a team — traveling thousands of miles to watch a game, spending thousands of dollars on apparel and other paraphernalia, painting their bodies and sitting shirtless in subzero weather, just to name a few of these behaviors. Recently, a company started marketing a special line of caskets — yes a person, if he so chooses, can be buried in a casket decorated with the colors and logo of his favorite team.

Sports, in general, have become a complex blend of business, law, criminology, psychology, and entertainment. With twenty-four-hour cable coverage, internet websites, full sections in hundreds of daily newspapers, general and specialty magazines, and sports radio, there is an almost endless supply of useless information being projected at even the most casual of fans.

Sometimes, I long for the simplicity of play and the merest basics of the game. That is what it is all about — who has won and who has lost — which is determined simply by who has scored the most points. In many sports, points are relatively easy to track. In soccer and hockey, for example, if the ball or puck goes into the net, the team scores. In baseball, if the base runner reaches home plate before there are three outs in an inning, it is a run — a point. Football, however, has the most complex scoring scheme of all the major sports — there are actions worth one point, two points, three points, and six points. The key unit is the touchdown worth six points, followed by the extra-point, worth one, which creates the combination of seven points on a successful scoring drive.

I do not think that the developers of the sport were thinking in biblical or religious terms when they devised the point system. They likely did not decide on the point total for a touchdown based on the six days of the week and Shabbat, the seventh day. Nevertheless, this quirk of scoring — six of something, followed by a seventh bonus or extra point — did trigger recognition of a pattern that shows a beautiful connection between a series of important mitzvot, seven of the most important biblical personalities, and the festival of Succot.

• • • HOME AND AWAY • • •

The festival of Succot stands out for many reasons. It is a festival of joy after the solemnity and weight of the Days of Awe. It represents the ongoing attention that God pays to our physical as well as spiritual well-being and the reciprocal trust that we place in Him. Finally, it is filled with some of the strangest rituals in our religion (at least to someone on the outside looking in). For seven days (or eight outside of Israel) we move out of our permanent homes and eat, sleep, and dwell in temporary huts covered with vegetation. On each of the days of Succot, while we recite important prayers, we hold, wave, and parade with a citron and a bunch of different leaves. On the seventh day, *Hoshanah Rabbah*, we hold a bunch of myrtle branches and hit the floor with them while reciting important prayers relating to repentance and forgiveness. The most important observance, and the one that gives the festival its name, is the requirement that we dwell in temporary huts — succot — in order to experience what it must have been like for the Jews who left Egypt.

But there is yet another special custom associated with Succot: *Ushpizin* (literally, guests). On each of the seven nights of succot we invite a very holy and special guest: Avraham, Yitzchak, Yaacov, Moshe, Aharon, Yosef, and David. The source of this custom is a passage from the mystical work, the *Zohar* (*Emor* 103b):

> When a man sits in the *tzila dimehemenuta* ("shade of faith," the succah) the *Shechinah* (Divine Presence) spreads its wings over him from above and Avraham and five other righteous ones and David make their dwelling with him.

The prayer book contains a prayer that combines the invitation and a request that God find favor with our observance of the mitzvah of succah.

Some may think that these are mere words — window dressing on the succah, if you will. Can we really take these "visits" seriously? Is this not just a variation on the visit that Eliyahu the prophet makes on the seder nights? Perhaps, but while most of us have not seen the Ushpizin literally, they nevertheless raise our consciousness of the holiness of the succah. Also, it is special to feel a connection, even if only through words and concepts with these men who shaped our heritage. As we will soon discover, we have other opportunities to visit with and interact with these guests.

HALL OF FAME

• • • CIRCUMCISION AND AVRAHAM • • •

There are six mitzvot in the Torah, the Rabbis teach us, that are meant to be fulfilled while standing. Not only are they linked by the way we fulfill them, but also thematically. All six mitzvot are described using the same word — "lachem," (for yourselves) — implying that they indeed have a deep connection to one another. In this section, I will argue that the six related mitzvot (circumcision, blowing the shofar on Rosh Hashanah, sactifying the new moon, *tzitzit*, Counting of the Omer, and shaking the *lulav)* are also related to the first six Ushpizin: Avraham, Yitzchak, Yaacov, Yosef, Moshe, and Aharon.

The first of the mitzvot we listed was circumcision. This mitzvah was first given to Avraham and represented a covenant (*brit*) with God and is so attached to Avraham that when we circumcise our sons to this day we declare in the text of the blessing that they are entering the Covenant of Avraham.

Acceptance of the covenant of circumcision is also listed among the ten tests that Avraham withstood on his path to greatness (*Pirkei Avot* 5:4).

Rabbi Moshe Feinstein (1895–1986) gives an insightful answer to a rather basic question regarding Avraham's action. The question is almost obvious: why was Avraham's acceptance of circumcision such a big deal? We perform this operation on newborn (eight-day-old) babies. This cutting of excess skin could not have been that intimidating to a mature and grown man, a man who challenged kings and armies, a man with the faith to challenge all of the world's prevailing philosophies and religions.

Reb Moshe observes that not only was it a great test, but it might have been the greatest test. The difficulty was not the action itself, but what it represented to Avraham. Essentially God seemed to be asking Avraham to do the one thing most fundamentally in contrast with his own nature.

From the narratives of the Torah we learn that Avraham was one of the most caring, concerned, and compassionate men of all time. He is famous for his kindness toward others. He risked his own life to save a family member, Lot, from whom he had previously separated, and debated with God to save cities filled with people who did not deserve compassion. Perhaps most important to him was his role as a proselytizer, reaching out to literally all of mankind in order to convert them to a monotheistic perspective.

Someone who is so completely a "people person" no doubt feels most effective when he can transcend or minimize any differences between himself and those with whom he is interacting. If he appears different or strange or fanatical, he will not have the same ability to influence and to simply perform acts of kindness. Up until the brit, Avraham likely thought of himself as one of the boys. Sure, he had different ideas, but in a sense that was the point — if he was one of the gang, yet accepted these ideas, then they must be OK. Now God was asking Avraham to mark himself physically. He would be noticed as being different. If so, it was possible that people would distance themselves from him. He might not receive the same acceptance. This troubled him so much, the Midrash relates, that before deciding to agree to the circumcision, Avraham actually took the first public opinion poll — consulting with his close friends Aner, Eshkol, and Mamre (*Bereishit Rabbah* 42:8). Nevertheless, he went ahead, had the brit, and passed the test.

• • • SHOFAR AND YITZHAK • • •

The next mitzvah is blowing the shofar on Rosh Hashanah. The Talmud, *Rosh Hashanah* 16a, asks why we sound the ram's horn. The answer is because God said: "Blow for Me the ram's horn that I may remember for you the binding of Yitzchak the son of Avraham, and I shall consider it as though you bound yourselves before Me."

The narrative of the binding of Yitzchak is one of the most famous and powerful in our entire religion, but one verse in particular illuminates this connection: "And Avraham raised his eyes and saw and behold a ram, afterwards, caught in the thicket by its horns; and Avraham went and took the ram and offered it as an offering in place of his son" (Gen. 22:13). The rabbis of the Midrash latch on to two seemingly superfluous sections of this verse to teach beautiful lessons. First, why is it significant that the ram was caught in the thicket by its horns?

Isn't it enough that Avraham saw a ram and offered it? Second, why does the verse state that Avraham offered it as an offering "in place of his son?" We know that Yitzchak was spared, so of course the offering is in place of his son! This clause does not impart new information.

The focus on the stuck horns is explained by Reb Yudin and Reb Yehudah ben Shimon as follows: "Through the generations of history, Israel will be captured in cycles of sin and persecution. However, in the end, they will be redeemed through the horn of the ram" (*Bereishit Rabbah* 56:9). In other words, the image that Avraham observes is a prophecy and promise for his children.

The extra phrase "in place of his son" is explained by Rabbi Pinchas as follows: "[Avraham] said, Master of the Universe, consider this act as if I had actually offered Yitzchak my son first and then I offered the ram" (*Bereishit Rabbah* 56:9). In other words, he was not asking that the ram replace Yitzchak. Rather, he was praying that Yitzchak retain the spiritual status of an offering — that he be considered of equal status with the ram that was actually sacrificed. As such, the shofar is more than just a tribute to Avraham's actions at the akeidah: it is the spiritual surrogate of Yitzchak.

• • • KIDDUSH HACHODESH AND YAACOV • • •

In the opening lines to his famous commentary on the Torah, Rashi tells us that the commandment of Sanctifying the New Moon (*Kiddush Hachodesh*) should have been the logical starting place for the Torah, since it is the first mitzvah that God gave to the Children of Israel. Rashi explains the nature of the command itself in his commentary on Exodus 12:2:

He [God] showed him [Moshe] the new moon and said to him, "When the moon renews, it shall be for you the beginning of the month." And a verse does not expand beyond its basic/textual meaning. Regarding the month of *Nisan*, He told him that this will be the first in the order of the counting of the months, *Iyar* will be called the second month, *Sivan* the third month, etc.

Thus, through God's command, the Jews established their own calendar. The procedures for determining the new month, for establishing specific dates and communicating when each month starts, as well as the method for determining when leap years are necessary in order to align the lunar-based 354-day Jewish calendar with the solar-based 365-day seasonal calendar, are all components of this mitzvah.

There are many opinions and explanations concerning why this was the first mitzvah. The most common approach is to relate it to the then-current status of the Jews as slaves. Slaves have little or no control over their own lives. This is most noticeable in the realm of time — they are not free to do things when they choose to do them. The parameters of time are set by the slave's master. One of the clearest signs of freedom for the Jews was, therefore, mastery over time. They set the calendar. The holiness of a holiday would be derivative of their ability to sanctify time, quite a powerful message for a nation enslaved!

So how does this mitzvah relate to Yaacov? The key to this link is the word for moon in Hebrew, *levanah* (*lamed-vet-nun-heh*), which is just the word *lavan* with the feminine *heh* at the end. Lavan is a word, but it is also the name of the father of Rachel and Leah. In the narratives of the book of Genesis, Lavan does not seem particularly evil or threatening. He seems portrayed as a sly and sneaky fellow — a snake oil or used car salesman. Yet, as we turn the pages of the *Haggadah* at our seder on Pesach we find the following proclamation: "Go and learn what Lavan the Aramean attempted to do to our father Yaacov. For Pharaoh decreed only against the males. Lavan attempted to uproot everything."

What we have here is not merely a link, but a deep message — Yaacov's experiences with Lavan are the paradigm or template for the experiences of his children in Egypt. On the most direct level we have broad thematic links. Yaacov, in order to preserve his physical well being, fled his home into exile in the house of Lavan. While there, he endured physical and psychological hardships in order to marry Rachel and yet he survived, multiplied, and prospered.

This completely foreshadows the experience of the Jews in Egypt. They initially descend to preserve their own well-being in the face of famine. They are enslaved in stages by trickery and changing conditions. They endure suffering, hardship, and wretchedness. They multiply at a miraculous rate, are saved through God's direct intervention, and depart with great wealth.

Let's turn back to the mitzvah of Kiddush Hachodesh. God certainly could have given the Jews any commandment at this point; He has six hundred and twelve others to choose from. But by focusing on the levanah, actually sanctifying time with the levanah, they symbolically and proudly connect with the heritage of their father Yaacov. They are enslaved, but will soon be freed. They are abused, but they will soon be wealthy. They are subjected to the corruption and immorality of Egypt, but now they are doing a mitzvah, one involving kid-dush, sanctification. When we stand for this mitzvah, we are able to stand because Yaacov showed us how.

• • • TZITZIT AND YOSEF • • •

The mitzvah of tziztit is one of the most symbolically pow-erful in the Jewish religion. When one places the required fringes on the corners of his garment, he is told "to see them and to remember all the commandments of God..." (Num. 15: 38). The connection between the tziztit and all six hundred thirteen commandments is rather direct. The numerical value, *gematria*, of the word tziztit is 600 (*tzadi*=90, *yud*=10, *tzadi*=90, *yud*=10, *tav*=400), plus the five knots and eight strings, total 613. However, the function of the tziztit is much more than a general catch-all reminder to do good. God established this mitzvah to combat man's propensity toward immorality. As the verse we quoted above continues, "...and you shall not turn after your heart and after your eyes after which you lust."

The story of Yosef is one of the most well known in the entire Torah. It has everything: high drama, passion, irony, symmetry, and a happy ending. We follow the life of Yosef as he progresses from a vain, immature dreamer to his ascension as the second most powerful man in the ancient world, next to the Egyptian Pharaoh. The narrative takes up the better part of four weekly portions, stretching from Chapters 37 to 50 of Genesis.

But despite his role in the story and the various episodes in his life, the Torah does not reveal much about the spiritual side of Yosef. We get a glimpse here of his immaturity, a splash there of his administrative expertise and wisdom and cunning. We also appreciate his adaptability and fortitude. Just imagine the inner strength he needed in order to endure the roller coaster ride that his life became. He succeeded as a slave and he succeeded as an aristocrat. Nevertheless, he is known in rabbinic literature not merely as Yosef, but as *Yosef Hatzaddik*, Yosef the Righteous.

The greatest challenge to Yosef's moral character was presented by the wife of his master, Potiphar. After being sold into slavery, Yosef soon impressed his master and became the chief of staff for his affairs. Potiphar's wife noticed the charismatic and handsome servant and approached him to be immoral with her.

Not only was Yosef a slave, he was a Hebrew, the lowest rung on the Egyptian social ladder, literally sold out by his family, alone, and likely looking for any opportunity to improve his lot. Rejecting the master's wife was not the way to make friends and win influence. Yet he does just that; he turns her down flat.

The first argument he makes is to claim loyalty to his master — his master trusts him and has invested him with so much authority, how can he violate it? But then he makes a more substantial argument, the one that reveals his inner character: "...how can I perpetrate this great evil and have sinned against God?" (Gen. 39:9). What an amazing statement! He is telling an Egyptian noblewoman, steeped in the idolatrous culture of Egypt, that he will not consent because he does not wish to sin before his God. To have such faith and to allow such faith to deter him from immorality is a true sign of righteousness.

Mrs. Potiphar, however, is not so easily dissuaded. She keeps at him day after day, cajoling, threatening, seducing, and nudging, but to no avail — Yosef will not succumb. Then one day, on an Egyptian religious holiday when no one else but Yosef would be home, she feigns an illness in order to pounce. She grabs him by his garment and demands that he lie with her.

> And she caught hold of him by his garment (*bigdo*) saying, "Lie with me"; but he left his garment (*bigdo*) in her hand and he fled and he went outside. When she saw that he had left his garment (*bigdo*) in her hand and fled outside.... (Gen. 39:12–13)

She then realizes that she has an opportunity to take revenge for the obvious humiliation that she is feeling. Standing there with Yosef's garment in her hand, she cries out until the other men of the household come running. She fabricates a version of the story, with Yosef as the aggressor using the garment as her proof. "She kept his garment (*bigdo*) beside her until morning" (Genesis 39:16). When her husband finally returns home, she again uses the garment: "And it was when I raised my voice and screamed, he left his garment (*bigdo*) beside me and ran outside" (Gen. 39:18).

There seems to be a lot of emphasis on Yosef's garment (*bigdo*). On one hand, this is rather ironic, since it could be said that a garment got him into this predicament in the first place. Yaacov showed that he held Yosef in higher esteem than the other brothers, and thus provoked their jealousy by giving him the famous Coat of Many Colors. But the word *beged* here ultimately references tzitzit, as we see by the use of the same word in Numbers 15:38: the tzitzit are made "on the corners of their garments (Bigdehem, *bet-gimel-dalet-yud-heh-mem sofit)* throughout their generations." (Numbers 15:38). Can you not hear the echo of Yosef's righteousness in this command? This is a command that references the beged that stands through generations, not only future, but perhaps past, as well, and that relates directly to resisting the temptation of immorality. This is the mitzvah of Yosef!

• • • COUNTING THE OMER AND MOSHE • • •

The time period of the Counting of the Omer, from the sixteenth of Nisan (the day after the first day of Pesach) through the fifth of Sivan (the day before Shavuot) has been a moving target of sorts throughout the generations. In its first incarnation it marked the forty-nine days between the exodus from Egypt and the revelation at Sinai. Later, it stood as a countdown between the offering brought in connection with the barley harvest (the Omer offering) and both the offering of the two loaves and the bringing of the first fruits, which are brought on Shavuot. After the destruction of the Second Temple, during the era of Roman persecution in the first half of the second century C.E., the Omer period became something very different — a period of mourning. "Rabbi Akiva had twelve thousand pairs of students, spread out all over the country from Gevat to Antipatros, and they all died during the short space of time between Pesach and Shavuot, because they did not treat each other with respect" (*Yevamot* 62b).

Finding the connection between Counting the Omer and Moshe as it relates to our initial encounter with this time period is rather simple. These forty-nine days were the very days that Moshe helped the Children of Israel cleanse themselves of the impurity of Egypt and to ascend the forty-nine levels of purity so that they could receive the Torah. The role of lawgiver and teacher was Moshe's most important purpose. We may identify Moshe with the exodus from Egypt, but on the very night that we discuss and celebrate the event, on the eve of the seder as we read the Haggadah, we find only one brief passing mention of Moshe, and that is in connection with the crossing of the Red Sea. Moshe had his part to play, but with regard to the redemption, we explain:

> God brought us out of Egypt — not through an angel, nor through a seraph, not through a messenger, but the Holy One Blessed Be He in His Glory, Himself, as it says; "I will pass through the land of Egypt on that night; I will slay all the firstborn of the land of Egypt from man to beast; and upon all of the gods of Egypt will I execute judgment, I God" (Haggadah text).

In fact, it could be argued that Moshe's "job" was not so much to free the Jews, as to teach them the Torah. If we turn back to Moshe's first encounter with God, at the burning bush, we find something interesting in the exchange. After God reveals Himself to Moshe and sets out the task, Moshe is reluctant. Displaying his great modesty, he does not believe himself capable or worthy: "Who am I that I should go to Pharaoh and that I should take the Children of Israel out of Egypt?" (Ex. 3:12). Rather than trying to impress Moshe with wonders and signs or even to reveal to him his historical destiny and impact, God answers, "...for I shall be with you — and this is your sign that I have sent you, when you take the people out of Egypt, you will serve God on this mountain" (Ex 3:13). In other words, the completion of Moshe's mission was not the physical redemption from Egypt. Rather, it was the service on this very mountain, this mountain of Sinai where Moshe would receive the Torah and transmit it to the people. Thus, the historical Counting of the Omer is linked to Moshe as the countdown to Torah, to the culmination of his mission.

We have to look a little more closely to find the connection between Moshe and the Omer, as first commanded in the Torah. But that, too, is amazingly direct. While the Children of Israel wandered in the desert, they received three special benefits. They received water from the well in the merit of Miriam. The Clouds of Glory surrounded them, protecting them, keeping them cool by day and warm at night, in the merit of Aharon. Finally, they were sustained by eating the manna, which could taste like anything they could imagine, in the merit of Moshe.

Each day every man, woman, and child received the portion necessary to sustain them for that day. They were not allowed to collect extra or to store it, other than on Fridays, when they collected a double portion for the Shabbat. How much manna is necessary to sustain a person? The Torah tells us as follows: "This is what God commands, collect of it each man according to his needs, *an Omer per head,* according to the number of people, each man shall collect for those in his tent" (Ex. 16:16). We now have a direct link between the Omer and the manna/Moshe.

However, there is one other command that God gave to

Moshe regarding the Omer that is perhaps the most convincing proof. Toward the end of Exodus Chapter 16 (verses 33–36) we find information that does not seem to fit. We have been cruising along since virtually the beginning of Genesis with a fairly straight historical chronology. In these verses, the Torah speaks of the covenant (the ark and tablets) and of the forty years in the desert. (Rashi, in his comment on verse 33, explains that God gave Moshe this command at a later point but the Torah included it here as it fit more logically with the manna topic.)

> This is the thing that God commanded; a full *Omer*
> of it shall be a safekeeping for your generations...
> Take one jar and put a full *Omer* of manna into
> it; place it before God for a safekeeping for your
> generations...Aharon placed it before the Ark of
> Testimony for safekeeping (Ex. 16:32–34).

Considering that we are associating the manna with Moshe and his merit, how fitting that it be placed with the Ark of Testimony that contains the two sets of tablets that Moshe brought from Sinai — the first broken ones and the second complete ones!

However, it is also interesting that even our current focus of the Omer period, the mourning we observe for the students of Rabbi Akiva, can be linked with Moshe. This is because, as we see in the Talmud (*Menachot* 29b), these two men are linked in the heavens as the greatest of teachers (Rabbi Akiva's students also appear in this narrative) and in a sense, they were both the teachers of these students.

The Talmud relates the following story: When Moshe

ascended to the heavens to receive the Torah, he found God attaching *tagin* (crowns) to the letters. Moshe asked why He was doing this. God replied, "After many generations there will arise a man, Akiva ben Yosef is his name, and he will expound on every little *kotz* (tittle) mounds and mounds of halachot." Moshe then asked to see this man. God told him to turn around. Moshe found himself in a study hall and he sat behind eight rows of Rabbi Akiva's students.

Moshe found that he was unable to follow the discussion and he felt inadequate. He finally experienced relief when they came to a certain subject and the students asked Rabbi Akiva what the source of a particular halachah was and Rabbi Akiva responded: "It is a law given to Moshe at Sinai."

Moshe then turned to God and said, "Master of the Universe, You have such a great man, yet You give the Torah through me?" God answered, "Be silent for this is My plan." Moshe then said, "Master of the Universe, You showed me his Torah, now show me his reward." God said: "Turn yourself around." Moshe turned and saw the Romans selling his flesh, which they had torn off his body with red hot metal combs, at the marketplace. Moshe said, "Master of the Universe, such Torah and this is the reward?" God answered, "Be silent for this is My plan."

Any way you look at it, when we count the Omer, we anticipate the Torah, we respect the Torah, we mourn the loss of Torah, and we prepare to receive the Torah. This, more so than any other, must be the time of Moshe.

• • • LULAV AND AHARON • • •

The mitzvah of *lulav* (palm branch) and *etrog* (citron) is one of the most mysterious in the Torah. We read: "You shall take for yourselves on the first day the fruit of a citron tree, the branches of the date palm, twigs of a plaited tree, and brook willows, and you shall rejoice before the Lord, your God, for seven days" (Lev. 23:40). But the question remains: What does this mitzvah represent and why these four species?

The Midrash offers a number of explanations, the following being one of the more widely accepted or well known:

'The fruit of a beautiful tree' — these are Israel. Just as the etrog has flavor and fragrance, so Israel has men who have Torah scholarship and good deeds. 'The branches of a date palm' — these are Israel. Just as the date palm has taste [the date fruit], but does not have fragrance, within Israel there are those who are accomplished in Torah scholarship, but do not have good deeds. 'Twigs of a plaited tree' — these are Israel. Just as the myrtle is fragrant but has no taste, so too within Israel are those that do good deeds but lack Torah scholarship. 'And brook willows' — these are Israel. Just as the willow has neither taste nor fragrance, so too among Israel are those devoid of Torah scholarship and good deeds. And what does God do with them? It would not be possible for Him simply to destroy them. Instead God said to tie them together in one binding, and they will atone for each other. Moreover, if they accomplish this, at that moment I will rise to honor you.... Therefore Moshe cautioned them 'to take for themselves on the first day'.... (*Vayikra Rabbah* 30:12).

This interpretation highlights just how powerful a symbol the four species are for our people. Not only do they represent each kind of Jew, but they highlight the responsibility that we have for each and every Jew — even those with no redeeming characteristics — no Torah and no good deeds! We are bound together. We are all limbs of the same body. If a finger is infected, you try to heal it — you would only amputate as a last resort.

But even beyond this shared responsibility is an amazing observation about the interconnectedness of the Jewish People. If those that are spiritually attuned show concern for their less pious brethren, if they include them in their prayers and in their own search for atonement, God will grant atonement to all. The binding and grouping of the four species represents an ideal of Jewish unity (not *the* ideal, which would be all joined together in perfect service of God). True concern for each other, unconditional concern, would result in peace for all.

No one was more of a living symbol of this ideal than Aharon. In *Pirkei Avot* 1:12, Hillel advises all of us: "Be among the disciples of Aharon, loving peace and pursuing peace, loving people and bringing them closer to Torah." This statement tells us a few things about Aharon. First and foremost is the fact that he was known as one who loved and pursued peace. Many stories are told of how Aharon intervened in all types of disputes between spouses, between friends, between business associates, in order to bring people back together. However, it is the second part of Hillel's statement that really clues us in to Aharon. If the people to whom he showed love were those with Torah and good deeds, there would not have been a need for him to bring them closer to Torah. They would have been there already — either through study or ethical practice. These were people who were far from Torah, yet they were loved by Aharon.

Aharon's role in the Torah often seems to be that of second fiddle. He goes with Moshe to Egypt as his spokesman; he stays behind when Moshe ascends to receive the Torah; he watches as Moshe hits the rock, etc. However, there was one area where he surpassed his younger brother. He, Aharon, was the *Kohen Gadol*, the High Priest. He performed the daily service in the *Mishkan* (Tabernacle), he lit the *Menorah* (candelabrum) each day, and only his children would be able to serve as priests. However, there was one service performed by the Kohen Gadol that surpassed all others in importance to the nation: the service on Yom Kippur, the Day of Atonement.

The rituals and procedures of that day are rather elaborate and the preparation for the Kohen Gadol was intense. However, he sought to accomplish the single most important task that anyone could perform for the Jews: atonement and forgiveness for all of their sins, literally taking the scarlet-stained fabric of the collective and cleansing it so that it appeared snow white. The Kohen Gadol did not perform these rituals and enter into the Holy of Holies just for the righteous or only for the masses of ordinary people. He sought atonement for all, even the worst sinners and heretics. If you were Jewish, the Kohen Gadol was your representative, down to the last Jewish man and woman. Aharon lived a life full of love for every Jew; it was only fitting that he be the one to represent them. Aharon figuratively walked around with the four species of Israel every day of his life, or better yet, he was the four species of the Jewish People — that was his personal philosophy.

• • • THE "EXTRA" POINT: DAVID • • •

We seem to be out of mitzvot, yet we have one tzaddik left. In terms of the metaphor we started with, we have our touchdown, but need the extra point! Like David himself, or more accurately what he represents, this point is at once hidden and obvious.

If you think back to our introduction to the Ushpizin, you will recall that the *Zohar* described them rather strangely — the six righteous ones *and David*. The intention is certainly not to imply that David is not righteous, but it does highlight that David is different from the others. Most obvious is the fact that he did not live in the historical timeframe of the Five Books of Moses, and thus is in another category. However, David represents much more than a fixed person or a time. David is almost a codeword with meaning in the past and in the future.

In the Grace after Meals on Succot we insert a short prayer, just one line, that hints at David's importance here: "The Compassionate One may He erect for us David's fallen booth (*Succat David Hanofalet*)." The term "David's fallen booth" has several possible meanings. It might be a reference to the Temple, which is called David's since he acquired the city of Yerushalayim in order to fulfill his ultimate dream to build it, paving the way for his son Shlomo to actually construct it. It could also be a prayer for the restoration of David's reign, i.e., the coming of Mashiach who will be a direct descendant of

David. Either way, the prayer reaches toward the future rather than the past, a future associated with David and his line.

While this is a future that we long for, it is one whose precise time is hidden from us. Rashi tells us as he describes Yaacov's last words to his sons: "Yaacov wanted to reveal the end of days to them, however the Divine Presence departed from him and he began to tell other things" (Rashi's comment on Gen. 49:1). In other words, it is literally before us, within our grasp, yet it is hidden. So too is David within our standing mitzvot — David, with his own fallen succah that must rise!

Recall that there was one word that connected all of these mitzvot and allowed the rabbis to apply the requirement of standing to each of them. The word was "lachem," for you, lamed-chaf-mem. The three letters of this word can be rearranged by putting the Mem first, then the Lamed, then the Chaf to spell...*MELECH*, KING, as in David *Hamelech*! David did not live early enough to be directly associated with any mitzvah of the Torah. However, the Torah is the blueprint for all of history, so it is not surprising to find that there could be such a direct reference, in this context, to David.

Just as the timing of the end of days is hidden from us, David's connection to the other Ushpizin is obscured, hidden, more of a hint. Nevertheless, our belief in the coming of the Mashiach and the rebuilding of the Temple is the platform upon which we sustain the belief structure established by the other six shepherds. In fact, the succah is the best metaphor for all of Jewish history — until Mashiach, everything is just a succah, a temporary dwelling. The First Temple was temporary. The Second Temple was temporary. The exile is long but temporary. The Third Temple will no longer be a succah, but home.

5

The Maccabees:
Secret Origins of Super Heroes
Chanukah

• • • INTRODUCTION TO SUPER HEROES • • •

In current pop culture, the super hero, a Jewish-American creation, is enjoying a renaissance and movies based on well-known characters like Superman and Batman are earning record box office receipts. These super-human characters appeal to the public in a number of ways. For some, they represent the comforting triumph of good over evil, the absolutely heroic in this confused post-September 11 society. Others find escape in the form of simple entertainment and still others, a more problematic retreat into fantasy. Finally, these heroes are substitutes for the myths and legends that the masses of mankind have historically clung to in the absence of a true belief system. Captain Marvel is a good example of this latter appeal.

Captain Marvel was one of the more interesting early heroes, developed by a rival publisher to capitalize on Superman's popularity. In the tale of his origin, a newsboy named Billy

Batson wandered down an abandoned tunnel and met an ancient wizard named Shazam. When he spoke the wizard's name, he magically changed into a powerful hero named Captain Marvel who had the wisdom of Solomon, the strength of Hercules, the stamina of Atlas, the power of Zeus, the courage of Achilles, and the speed of Mercury.

But there is an incongruity among these six components of Captain Marvel's power: one is not like the other five. As we know, Solomon (Shlomo) was a real person — a king, a prophet, a holy man who built the first *Beit Hamikdash* (Holy Temple) in Yerushalayim. The other figures are mythological figures and false gods. However, this can allow us to appreciate that many biblical and historic figures that are parts of Jewish tradition are not merely heroic. By virtue of their superior wisdom or strength or prowess in battle (all gifts from God, of course), they qualify as "super heroes." These heroes likewise have tales of origin, a source for their power and motivation. In this chapter, we will explore the origins of one of the mightiest groups of Jewish heroes, the Maccabbees, who stood against the might of the Greek-Assyrians and rededicated the Beit Hamikdash, Solomon's first Holy Temple, in 139 BCE, and discover their "connections" to other events and personalities of Jewish history.

• • • What is History? • • •
How to Approach Chanukah

For secular academics and scholars, history is the past. They study it using physical artifacts (archaeology), contemporaneous writings, and the recorded observations of historians and scholars from earlier eras. History is a linear progression, moving back in a straight line to the events and personalities and moving forward to our perspectives and environment.

As we approach the study of history as a religious exercise by introducing God into the equation, these lines do not simply blur — they disappear completely. God is infinite and timeless. The letters of very name of God that we do not pronounce, Y-H-V-H, can be rearranged to spell the words *hayah, hoveh, yihyeh* (was, is, will be). This stresses to us that for God, everything is essentially in the here and now, the present. God is creating the world at this moment. He *is* taking the Jews out of Egypt, He *is* giving the Torah, and He *is* bringing Mashiach. In a God-centered view of history, every event is part of a plan, and it may well be linked to other events, actions, and personalities that will take place centuries later.

Thus, while we could view the story of Chanukah and the actions of the Maccabees in isolation — a revolution by a group of courageous men (religious fundamentalists) who used guerilla tactics against powerful and oppressive Hellenistic/secular authorities and managed to reestablish tradition and a Jewish monarchy — we will instead view the event within the context of its religious origins and show how it was the culmination of preordained spiritual forces that were placed in motion at the time of the initial creation of the world. Tracing these sources takes on great significance especially because there is no scriptural account of the story of Chanukah and there is scarce discussion of the holiday in Talmudic literature.

• • • EARLY ORIGINS • • •

Commenting on Numbers 8:2, the Yerushalayim Talmud asks:

> Why is the portion of *Beha'alotchah* [the portion we
> read on Chanukah] placed next to the dedication
> of the altar? Because when the princes of the twelve
> tribes brought their offerings for the dedication, the
> Levites anguished for they had not brought any-
> thing. God thus said to Moshe, "Speak to Aharon
> and tell him, 'When you kindle the lights' [which
> is a promise that] they will participate in another
> dedication that of the sons of Matityahu the high
> priest and the sons of Chashmonai."

This Midrash is an example of the God-centered view of
history. An event that will take place hundreds of years in the
future, which continues to resonate by way of commemoration and practice in the present, is the response to a concern
that Aharon and the tribe of Levi had in the distant past. This
Midrash also links several important themes that provide clues
to the origins of the Maccabees, namely, the role of the tribe of
Levi, the role of the *kohanim* (priests, descended from Aharon),
and the dedication of the Mishkan.

In a Midrash on Genesis 2:2 (*Bereishis Rabbah* 2:4) we
see that the second verse of the Torah — "When the land was
tohu (unformed) and *vohu* (void), with *choshech* (darkness)
upon the surface of the *tehom* (deep), and the Divine Presence
merachefet (hovered) upon the surface of the waters" — actually presents us with a roadmap of history. Rabbi Shimon
ben Lakish explains that the four characteristics of the world
before God began to create anything correspond to the four
major periods of history, also known as the four exiles. *Tohu* relates to Babylon, *vohu* to Media, *choshech* to Greece, and *tehom*

to Rome. Finally, the Divine Presence hovering represents the eventual end of exile and the coming of Mashiach.

Greece is the third kingdom and it represents darkness. The Shem MiShmuel explains (*Chanukah Leil 7, shnat trp"g d"h vneira*) that this darkness represents the fact that Greece added its own evil to the proficiency of the evils perfected by the Babylonian and Persian kingdoms. Greece fostered paganism like Babylonia and immorality like Persia. It then added a dimension of butchery and murder (think of the story of Channah and her sons) to complete the triumvirate (idolatry, immorality, and murder). To combat the influence of a regime that cultivated the three cardinal sins required a tribe that had displayed the fortitude and zeal to stand against all three. Based upon precedential action, that tribe was Levi.

This Midrash (*Bereishis Rabbah* 99:2) describes that Yaacov and Moshe each designated counterbalances or antidotes for each period of exile from among the tribes: Yehuda against Babylonia, Binyamin against Persia, Yosef against Rome, and Levi against Greece. The Midrash likewise explains the characteristic or merit that would allow each of these tribes to prevail. However, the primary characteristics that define Levi's link to Greece seem rather flimsy: "This is the third tribe and this is the third kingdom, this has three letters in its name and this has three letters in its name." What is the point of this Midrash and what are the special characteristics of Levi?

The first time we encounter Levi, aside from his naming by Leah, is when he is thirteen years old and he and his brother Shimon act to avenge the rape of their sister Dena at the hands of Shechem, the son of a local tribal leader. As the incident is recounted in Genesis 34, Yaacov and his family return to the land of Canaan from Paddan-Aram, reconcile with Esav, and establish a homestead in Shechem, which he purchases from Chamor. Shechem, the son of Chamor, notices Dena, desires her, rapes her, and kidnaps her. When Yaacov is informed of the incident, he chooses not to take action before consulting with his sons. But when the sons return from the day's labors and hear what happened to their sister, they are morally outraged (Gen. 34:7). From the narrative it seems that they agree to negotiations that would lead to a merger between the two families and cultures, rather than revenge and retribution. The men of Shechem undergo circumcision as proof of their sincerity.

However on the third day of their recovery, Levi and Shimon take up their swords and massacre every male in the city. Yaacov seems genuinely upset at the actions of Levi and Shimon and rebukes them (Gen. 34:30). They defend themselves by responding that their zeal was warranted as the proper response to immorality. "Should he treat our sister like a harlot?" (Gen. 34:31). This seems to be the last word on the subject.

Many decades later, when Yaacov is on his deathbed in Egypt, he summons his sons in order to bless them before he dies. As we review his words in Genesis 49, we note that some of the sons receive explicit blessings while others receive veiled prophecies and still others, including Shimon and Levi, are rebuked.

> Shimon and Levi are brothers; their weaponry is a stolen craft. Into their conspiracy may my soul not enter, with their congregation, do not join. Accursed is their rage for it is intense and their wrath for it is

harsh, I will separate them within Yaacov and I will disperse them in Israel (Gen. 49:5–7).

From this we learn that Levi's capacity for violence and revenge, whether justified or not, and despite its origin in his intolerance for immorality, is to be punished for many generations to come.

The next time Levi is mentioned separately in the Bible is in Exodus 2:1–2: "A man went from the house of Levi and he took a daughter of Levi. The woman conceived and gave birth to a son. She saw that he was good and she hid him for three months." This, of course, refers to the birth of Moshe, our most important leader and teacher. When Moshe is born, the Torah tells us little specific information about his mother or father, not even their names, even though they are great and courageous people in their own right. We are likewise told little of his childhood and upbringing other than the fact that he was rescued from the waters of the Nile by a daughter of Pharaoh (Ex. 2:5–10) and is then presumably raised by her.

The very first time the Torah describes the adult Moshe is the day he goes out among his brothers and witnesses an Egyptian man striking a Hebrew man in a life threatening manner. Rather than acting as an Egyptian and accepting or ignoring the violence, the Torah relates: "He turned this way and that way and saw that there was no man, so he killed the Egyptian and he hid him in the sand" (Ex. 2:12). This man, Moshe, is a Levite through and through. Interestingly, we first learn about his character from a violent action and its aftermath. Like his grandfather Levi, Moshe can kill. This time, however, the provocation is not immorality. Moshe acts to prevent the spilling of Jewish blood.

Thus, the Torah portrays Moshe as a man who does not fear using lethal force in the face of conflict and who seeks to confront threats head-on rather than through diplomacy or even strategic retreat. However, when the Torah punctuates this act with an encounter Moshe has the very next day with two Jews who are fighting, we soon discover that we have jumped to an overly simple conclusion about him. Moshe is not a hothead or a madman. Quite the contrary, he seems to abhor violence — even calling the Jew who strikes his fellow "wicked" (Ex. 2:13). While these Hebrews diffidently talk back to Moshe, going so far as to denigrate his heroic action of the previous day, Moshe merely retreats. When this son of Levi is confronted with the injustice of a cardinal sin, he can defy convention, risk all, and act decisively, despite the fact that he is by nature peaceloving and nonconfrontational. In fact, this nonconfrontational aspect of his personality is highly praised when denominated as modesty.

From the point in time (and biblical narrative) when God gives Moshe the task of dealing with Pharaoh, until the initial revelation at Sinai, Moshe deals with confrontation calmly. In fact, he seems rather passive in the face of the initial challenges to his authority — first, when the Jews hesitate to enter the Red Sea and later when they complain about the lack of food and water. In both instances God acts and tells Moshe precisely what to instruct the people. In contrast, when Moshe confronts the reality and the magnitude of the sin of the Golden Calf, he acts decisively and harshly. He not only throws down and breaks the tablets containing the Ten Commandments that God had just fashioned, but he orders that the Golden Calf be melted down and that the ashes be mixed with water which he gives to the Children of Israel to drink.

One would think that these actions might have provided enough of an outlet for Moshe's anger. However, he turns to his brother Aharon, who appeared to be somewhat complicit in forging the idol, and grills him with a rather pointed question: "Moshe said to Aharon, 'What did this people do to you that you brought a terrible sin on it?'" (Ex. 32:21). When Aharon explains the circumstances — the mob mentality, his attempts to delay the action, and the risk to his own life — Moshe gains an even deeper understanding about the disgrace of the nation and how the cancer of idolatry, a consequence of their prolonged exposure to Egyptian culture, threatened the nation in its infancy. He recognizes that he must take drastic action, rather than directly calling for Divine retribution of one sort or another. He could not take the required action by himself so he calls out for compatriots using the slogan later co-opted by Matityahu in his struggle against the Greeks: "Whoever is for God, join me" (Ex. 32:26). It is then the tribe of Levi that gathers around Moshe ready to act.

We soon discover what the act is to be:

> And he said to them, "So has the Lord the God of Israel said, every man should put his sword on his thigh and pass back and forth from gate to gate in the camp and let every man kill his brother, every man his fellow, every man his relative" (Ex. 32:27).

In seeking to understand why the tribe of Levi steps forward to uphold Divine honor, but also to engage once again in killing, the Midrash comments:

Just as the third day of creation represents the separation of the waters, after which the waters gathered in one place, so with Levi, the third born. Moshe called out, "Whoever is for God, join me," and the tribe of Levi joined him (*Midrash Tadshei* 21).

The threat posed by the Golden Calf and the actions of the mixed multitudes involved confusing the Jews and enticing them towards idol worship. Levi acted completely within character by responding to Moshe's call to arms. However, notwithstanding the very Levi-like action of the tribe in responding to challenge, the actions of Aharon, the very prince of the tribe, stand out as facilitating rather than impeding the creation of the Golden Calf.

Rabbi Shimon Schwab (*Me-ayn Bais Hashoeva*, p.363, *Pinchas*) gives a fascinating insight into Aharon's actions by the sin of the Golden Calf. He comments that the essence of Aharon, as described in *Pirkei Avot* (1:12), is that "he loved and pursued peace, loved his fellowmen and sought to bring them closer to the Torah." While not a passive person, his behavior was guided by compassion and empathy. When the people gathered against him and demanded that he fashion the idol, his innate compassion overwhelmed his zealotry and he thus could not motivate himself to the level of zeal and self-sacrifice displayed by his nephew Chur. Thus when the Calf emerged from the fire, a slight taint likewise emerged to the status of Aharon's priesthood.

Because of Aharon's actions regarding the Golden Calf, it is only his grandson Pinchas who not only reinforces most directly the characteristics of Levi, but who transmits them forward across millennia to the Maccabees, despite the fact that he was initially denied the priesthood. Although he is the grandson of Aharon and the son of the high priest Elazar, his mother was a daughter of Yitro, who was also known as a priest among idolatry, and so the rabble-rousers of the time often labeled Pinchas with the pejorative, *"ben putiel,"* son of idol worshippers.

But in the thirty-ninth year after the exodus from Egypt, during the plotting of Balak the King of Moav and Bilaam the evil prophet against the Jewish People, Pinchas will prove himself. As the crisis unfolded, the Jews were poised to enter and to conquer the Land of Israel (then known as Canaan). The elders of Midian and Moav were intimidated by the strength of the Jews and feared that they would be conquered and so they hired the evil prophet Bilaam to curse the Jews. God, however, would not allow this to happen. Bilaam is ultimately forced to admit to his patron, "If Balak were to give me his houseful of silver and gold, I would not be able to transgress the word of God to do good or bad on my own. Whatever God speaks, that I shall speak" (Num. 24:13).

Nevertheless, either out of sheer wickedness or merely out of a desire to earn his promised reward, Bilaam is still not willing to submit. Even after God forces him to bless rather than curse the Jews, Bilaam, with the able assistance of Balak, hatches a nefarious plot. They unleash a bevy of attractive females to entice the Jewish men to sin and to lead them to idol worship. The Midianites give this mission such high priority, that they even send their king's own daughter, Kozbi.

As the incident unfolds, the women are successful in their attempt to corrupt the Jews. Jewish men publicly weaken and engage in immoral conduct and idol worship. The mood is so overwhelming that Zimri son of Salu, the prince of the tribe of Shimon, is among those caught in this net of iniquity. Order breaks down and, as a consequence, a plague breaks out. Soon God's wrath is striking down the Jewish People, and the leadership, including Moshe, seems paralyzed.

If we freeze the scene, it is worth pausing to examine some of the dynamics in play. All three of the cardinal evils are loose — Jews are engaged in immoral conduct and idol worship, and death is everywhere. While the Torah reveals little about the identities of the sinning Jews, the one notable is — the prince of Shimon. This is in contrast with the historical Shimon who, with his brother Levi, wiped out Shechem to punish their immorality. Finally, the known and proven leaders, men like Yehoshua and Calev, who showed no compunction in the past to face off against rebellious elements (they ideologically took on the spies even though they were outnumbered) are absent. From where will the salvation come?

At this point, Pinchas the son of Elazar the son of Aharon the kohen decides to take action. He sees that the mighty, the zealous, the leaders — Yehudah, Binyamin, etc. — are silent and not willing to defend God's Honor. He also understands that there are times that responsibility demands action. The action he takes is violent and decisive. He jams a spear through the two human symbols of the corruption, Zimri and Kozbi, while they are carnally engaged. Pinchas's act, as violent and gory as it appears, is a culmination of all that he is. As a true Levite, he is predisposed to acting when zeal is required and God's honor is so publicly at stake. But this violence is not blood lust — it is actually something more akin to compassion. Pinchas is a descendant of Aharon. The Torah, when it identifies him, links him back two generations to his grandfather, rather than just to his father Elazar. The purpose is to link the two men and to show that their primary actions had the same result, to cool God's wrath. Aharon did this by offering incense (something he also did in his role of confronting Korach and the two hundred fifty men who rebelled with him against the authority of Moshe and Aharon). Pinchas used violence to stop even greater violence.

Rabbi Schwab describes the connection between Aharon and Pinchas, their fundamental characteristics and defining actions, even more directly. He suggests that Aharon was so compassionate and peace-loving that he was not able to fully cope with the events of the Golden Calf incident as they unfolded. As a true son of Levi, the requisite zeal coursed through his veins and he, perhaps, may have felt an urge to act in a manner similar too his nephew Chur, who sacrificed his own life in a futile attempt to halt the Jews' sinful conduct. However, rather than acting, he held back — he simply cared too much, he loved his people too much.

When the dust settled, God established the concepts of the Mishkan and the *Kehunah* (Priesthood). God bestowed the priesthood on Aharon and his sons and Moshe anointed them for this duty. However, in light of the slight flaw in Aharon's actions, there was a flaw in this appointment. While Aharon and his four sons became kohanim, and while this appointment was extended to future generations, it did not affect those descendants, like Pinchas, who were extant but whom Moshe did not anoint with the oil. When Pinchas responded zealously and with the required violence, he repaired or compensated for the initial deficiency in Aharon's character, thus earning the priesthood and restoring the family honor. Moreover, his actions, perhaps more so than any of the previous "Levite" actions, resonate into the future. God proclaims, "And it shall be for him and his children after him a covenant of *eternal* priesthood because he took vengeance for God and he atoned for the Children of Israel" (Num. 25:13).

Lest we think that this act is one of pure savagery, God immediately bestows another reward on Pinchas that itself characterizes the act and its motives: "Behold I bestow upon him My covenant of peace" (Num. 25:12). God is, in a sense, placing an imprinter on Pinchas's actions — that of peace. The Sifri comments on this gift: "This teaches that there descended from him eighteen High Priests in the First Temple era and eighty in the Second Temple era." In other words, all of the High Priests of the two Temple eras, including Matityahu and his sons, are linked to Pinchas and Levi.

The final biblical note regarding Levi, and perhaps the most fitting transition as we telescope history to the time of the Maccabees, is delivered by Moshe in his closing remarks to the Jewish People. As he stands at Arvot Moav offering blessing and prophetic insights to the Children of Israel, he proclaims: "Of Levi he said…Bless, O God, his army and favor the work of his hands, smash the loins of his foes and his enemies, that they may not rise" (Deut. 33:8 and 11). Rashi comments:

> He saw that in the future Chashmonai and his sons would battle against the Greek/Assyrians and he prayed for them for they were few — the twelve sons of Chashmonai and Elazar against a multi-

tude of thousands. Therefore it says, "Bless, O God, his army and favor the work of his hands."

This is even more direct than the promise God made to Aharon regarding the Menorah and the miracle of the oil. The descendants of Levi are not only destined to battle the Greek/Assyrians, physically and spiritually. They will battle against extreme odds — the few against the many. Perhaps as few as a dozen or so would be battling against thousands. What then actually happened, from a spiritual/historical perspective? How did these elements actually combine?

• • • THE HEROES OF CHANUKAH • • •

The festivals of Chanukah and Purim form an interesting unit. They share many common characteristics – the *"Al Hanissim"* prayer, a quasi-holiday status, and the very fact that we identify them as Rabbinic holidays. There are also significant differences. Many commentators define this contrast by associating Chanukah with the obligation to "give thanks and to praise," and Purim with "feasting and rejoicing." The two holidays also have quite different rituals. The centerpiece of Chanukah is the menorah lighting, while on Purim the most important observance is the reading of the *Megillah*, the "Scroll of Esther," a book of the Bible that provides a relatively contemporaneous account of the events in Shushan. The Chanukah story has no such text.

This distinction did not escape the notice of the sages of the Talmud as is seen in the following:

> Rav Assi said: "Why is Esther compared with the morning? To tell you just as the morning is the end

of the night, so too Esther (the events of Purim) represents the end of all (redemptive) miracles. But there is (the miracle of) Chanukah? However, Purim was the last miracle that was allowed to be recorded as part of the written scriptures" (Yoma 29a).

This is not to say that the story of Chanukah and its details have been lost or obscured. The events of this era were recounted by Josephus, appear as a book of Apocrypha, are included in a number of talmudic narratives, have been transmitted in the form of a number of midrashim, and are the subject of a work, *Megillat Antiochus* (the Scroll of Antiochus), that may have been written by the surviving sons of Matityahu as a record of what they experienced.

Without a definitive text, we are thus left with this range of different texts that provide varying details. Was the king involved or was it a general or a governor? How many soldiers engaged in the various battles? Who started the revolt, under what circumstances, and when? However, collectively these sources establish the context of the Greek exile. The narratives contain many similar elements, elements that resonate with the characteristics highlighted in the midrashim describing this exile. We find examples of religious persecution (immorality and brutal murder). Likewise there are tales of both national and individual faith and courage. Echoing the Book of Esther, Jewish women and their heroism play a prominent role in the description of events.

The first version of the *Midrash Ma'aseh Chanukah* contains the tale of a woman, identified as Channah, the daughter of Matityahu the high Priest. On the day of her wedding she was to be delivered first to the local governor. Many of the Jewish scholars and dignitaries had gathered for the celebration. As they gathered, she entered the room, pounded on the table to attract their attention, and proceeded to remove her gown. As she stood naked before the now-uncomfortable crowd, a few offended participants rose to strike her down. Before this could happen she shouted:

> Listen my brothers and friends! You act so zealously and self-righteously because I stand naked before you, despite the fact I am innocent of any sin. Yet you display no such passion or zeal knowing that you will shortly be turning me over to the uncircumcised who will defile me? You need to learn from Shimon and Levi, the brothers of Dena, who despite being only two in number, acted zealously on behalf of their sister and killed out the city of Shechem and risked their lives for God's Honor.

Needless to say, her five brothers and others from among the families of priests who were in attendance met the challenge and successfully rebelled against the immediate threat of their oppressor. The courage, strength of purpose, and very character of their ancestor infused their very beings and influenced their actions. The events are linked spiritually and textually. Channah did not merely use the name of Levi as an example; in actuality she was reminding all those present — all of the kohanim who were his descendants — that they were "programmed" to respond to this situation.

Megillat Antiochus provides another example of how those involved with the events of Chanukah understood, accessed, and used this "Levi-programming." The book sets the stage by describing the cruelty of the Greek king and the formidability of the General Bagrit with his huge army and war elephants. As a prelude to the conflict, Matityahu gathers his five sons to bless them and to motivate them for the overwhelming task before them:

> And their father blessed them and said: "Yehudah, my son, may you be steeled like Yehudah the son of Yaacov, who is compared to a lion. Shimon, my son, I liken you to Shimon the son of Yaacov who killed the residents of Shechem. Yochanan, my son, I give you the ability of Avner the son of Ner, the Commander in Chief of the Armies of Israel (in the time of King David). Yonatan, my son, I make you like Yonatan the son of Shaul, who fought against a savage enemy. Elazar my son, be like Pinchas the Son of Elazar, who was zealous for God and brought atonement upon the Children of Israel."

Of course, they all had within them the power of Levi. Matityahu was not playing the role of the sorcerer Shazam. He was reminding each of his sons of the spiritual power that coursed through their veins. The power of Shimon and Levi and Pinchas and Moshe and all of their spiritual progenitors and ancestors was part of their spiritual/genetic makeup. They simply needed to be reminded — be it by Matityahu or by their sister — of the existence of this super power within them. Do we have this latent ability? The evidence would suggest that we do, if we believe strongly enough.

CHAPTER

6

Who Knows Ten?

The Connections Between Pesach, Purim, and Shavuot

• • • ASKED AND ANSWERED • • •

In life everything is either good or evil. What you read and hear is either true or false. Our choices are always clear-cut — there is the path you should take and the one you should not take. How many of you wish it were all that simple?

In reality, most everything is ambiguous. How we comprehend a situation or size up a person is based on experience, education, instinct, and blind chance. However, we can often improve the odds by observing first and then asking the right questions. If we have more information we can avoid mistakes and pitfalls. But, it is not so easy to ask questions, especially the right questions. A person's inquisitiveness is sometimes overpowered by ego (not wanting to appear uninformed), limited knowledge, or attitude. On Pesach we get a glimpse of this as we take note of the approaches taken by the four sons to the rituals of the evening. We have scholarly depth, mocking cynicism, simple curiosity, and ignorant muteness.

Jews like questions. We certainly do questions a lot better than we do answers. Our belief structure is built on a foundation of faith — questions that we can ask but cannot always answer. For example: If God knows everything that will ever happen how can we have free will? Why do the righteous suffer and many evil-doers prosper? What was the nature of existence before creation? What will the world be like after the Mashiach arrives? What is the nature of our existence after death? These questions grasp at core beliefs like Divine reward and punishment, God's infinite Being, the coming of Mashiach, and the resurrection of the dead. The answers, however, may well be beyond our comprehension.

Then there are the questions that regularly torment and frustrate us: Why were so many killed in the Holocaust, including one million children? Why have so many innocent men, women, and children who live such passionate lives in our holy Land of Israel been victimized by hateful murderers? How do the terrorists of the world, the Bin Ladens and the Saddam Husseins and the Arafats, survive setback after setback and continue to undermine decency? To these questions, we do not possess any answers, or at least any satisfying answers. We can only maintain the core belief that God is in charge and thus there must be reason — a method to the madness.

These sorts of existential questions are fundamentally what Pesach and Purim are about. So many things seem to be spinning out of control for the Jewish People. They are enslaved and the evil idol worshippers are calling the shots, even murdering babies. Or they face a pogrom of massive almost universal proportion and seem defenseless. They cry out and question. Where are the answers? What could these answers possibly be?

These are the holidays of questions that lead to real, satisfying answers. This is why, especially on Pesach, we emphasize questions. We may start our seder by asking the Four Questions. However, if we are interested in teaching and learning and if we are interested in experiencing something more than a good meal with family and friends, then we should be raising and answering dozens of questions. By analyzing, seeking, and discussing, we may come closer to discovering the patterns and connections that lead to the answers that we seek.

Following this reasoning, I want to establish the connections between Pesach and Purim by posing a series of questions — some familiar, others a bit obvious, yet others somewhat sublime.

• • • A FEW GOOD QUESTIONS • • •

Near the end of the *Haggadah* we sing the famous riddle song *"Echad Mi Yode'ah"* (Who knows one?). We do not know who wrote this song; however, it has appeared in Hagaddot since the fifteenth century. A few number-related questions come to mind immediately when we think of Pesach. For example:

- Who knows two? Two are the Tablets of the Covenant Who knows ten? Ten are the Ten Commandments. Is this not the same answer? Why the repetition?

- Considering that this is Pesach, is there not another "ten" that is relevant and rather impressive — the Ten Plagues? While we are mentioning them, let us raise the question: why were there *ten* plagues?

- As we examine the two tablets or Ten Commandments,

something should strike us as odd, right from the outset. God makes His grand entrance by stating: "I am the Lord, your God, Who has taken you out of the land of Egypt, from the house of slavery." That is certainly impressive. However, would it not have been even more impressive if He had said, 'I am the Lord, your God, Creator and Master of the Universe,' or something along those lines?

As we know, the festival of Purim occurs in the month of Adar. The Talmud (*Megillah* 6b) discusses the issue of whether we read the Megillah on the fourteenth day of the first Adar or of the second Adar during a leap year. Rabbi Eliezer the son of Reb Yosi argues that it is the first one and Rabban Shimon ben Gamliel says it is the second. Our normative practice here follows the opinion of Rabban Shimon ben Gamliel, based on the reason, "we want to connect redemption to redemption." As Rashi explains, the motivation is to connect the redemption of Purim with that of Pesach (the month of Shevat, which precedes the first Adar has no such connection). This leads us to pose a few crucial questions about Purim:

- What is the redemption associated with Purim? There may well have been a salvation — the Jews avoided a pogrom — but, at the conclusion of the incident, they remained in exile as subjects of the Persians.
- In the Haggadah text, in a poem entitled, "and you shall say, this is the Feast of Passover" (*Va'amartem Zevach Pesach*), we read the line: "You caused the head of the evil clan (Haman) to be hanged on a fifty cubit gallows on Pesach." Where does this link come from?
- What does redemption even mean in this context?

• • • TORAH IS ALWAYS THE ANSWER • • •

The path to all of the answers, like most paths, starts at the beginning. You generally cannot officially reach the finish line if you did not begin at the starting line — even if you wish to try a few shortcuts. To find our answers, we literally must start at the very beginning, all the way back to the creation of the world.

The *Mishnah* in *Pirkei Avot* 5:1 states:

> With ten utterances the world was created. What does this come to teach us? Indeed, could it not have been created with one utterance? This was to exact punishment from the wicked who destroy the world that was created with ten utterances, and to bestow goodly reward upon the righteous who sustain the world that was created by ten utterances.

This Mishnah requires some explanation, and yes, it does raise a few questions of its own.

What are the utterances that are referenced here? The word for utterance, *ma'amar*, is derived from the root *amar*, *aleph-mem-resh*, to say. God did not create the world through action but through speech. We acknowledge this in our daily prayers when we proclaim, "*Baruch she'amar vehayah ha'olam*" (Blessed is He Who spoke and the world came into being). If you review the first chapter of Genesis, which contains the narrative of the first week of creation, you should find that God created by "saying" ten times (e.g., Gen. 1:3: "And God said 'Let there be light,' and there was light"). But, actually, if you review the creation story, you will find only nine occurrences of a Divine "saying." How then can the sages state that there

111

were ten?

The Talmud in Rosh Hashanah, 32a, discusses this very question:

> "With ten utterances the world was created." What are they? [If you count] "And He said" in the portion of Bereishit there are only nine? "*Bereishit*" [the first word, 'In the beginning'] is also an utterance, as it is written (Tehillim 33): "The world was [initially] created with the Word of God."

The term "Bereishit" is an utterance in and of itself. The fact that the Torah does not signify this by using an *Aleph-Mem-Resh* verb is because this one utterance was qualitatively different from the other nine. Before *Bereishit*, there was nothing — absolute and total nothing (the Hebrew term for this is *ayin*). In other words, at one moment there was zero and the next there was "heaven and earth," a substantive reality (in Hebrew, *yesh*). From that time forward, all subsequent creation was built upon this *yesh*. Essentially, the next nine steps involved God directing or saying something to the *yesh*.

So why did God not merely say "abracadabra," or in this case "bereishit," and let the completed world emerge? Was there really any difference for God? Do ten utterances require more effort than one? As the first Mishnah we quoted explains, the utterances have to do with reward and punishment, as well as the righteous and the wicked.

When God created the world, the most unique aspect within His most unique creation was man's free will. God is all-knowing, and all-powerful. There is no existence in heaven or earth separate from that of God. Nevertheless, God carved out one place that gives everything its character, that makes it all interesting, that makes this a world full of people rather that automatons that are compelled to do God's Will. That place is the portion of man's soul where he can exercise choice. Man should do what God wants. But man can make other choices. If man chooses correctly, then he is righteous. If he chooses the other path, he is wicked.

If someone knew with absolute and unshakeable certainty that there is a God, that He is always aware of what we do and that He controls all, then it would be nearly impossible to violate His will. When that awareness comes as a result of self-awareness, study, and discipline — the result is a tzaddik. If, however, the knowledge comes as a result of God speaking to a person or constantly and openly displaying His miracles and Presence — it is no big deal if that person is righteous.

The point that the Mishnah is making is that if God had created the world with one amazing flourish, no one would be able to doubt His mastery, His Existence, or His Presence. There would be no righteous or wicked. Instead, there would just be a world full of spiritually aware people. The ten utterances, like the passage of six days, represents process — evolution and the laws of nature. If you look for God, as Avraham did, you can reach no other conclusion than the fact that there is one God Who is Master of all. However, if you would like to believe otherwise, to delude yourself and to worship artifice rather that Godliness, then you can choose to hide God behind the curtain of process.

Thus the number ten, in and of itself, is not necessarily significant, even in this context. It seems that it is used to represent the concept of a complete system; the ten sayings represent the process of creation, Avraham's ten tests represent his spiritual ascension, the Ten Commandments represent the complete unit of Torah, and of course the ten plagues represent the complete process of breaking down the Egyptians. God used the process of ten utterances to obfuscate His involvement with creation and the ongoing existence of the world in order to nurture free choice. However, just as He used ten layers of process to hide His Presence, when the time came for Him to make Himself known, He had to remove these very layers. This act of uncovering can be observed in the narrative of the Ten Plagues.

Immediately before the first plague of blood, God says to Moshe:

> You shall speak everything that I shall command you, and Aharon your brother shall speak to Pharaoh, that he should send the Children of Israel from his land. But I shall harden Pharaoh's heart and I shall multiply My signs and My wonders in the land of Egypt. Pharaoh will not heed you, and I shall put My Hand upon Egypt; and I shall take out my legions — My people the Children of Israel — from the land of Egypt with great judgments. *And Egypt shall know that I am God,* when I stretch out My Hand over Egypt and I shall take the Children of Israel out from among them" (Ex. 7:2–5).

In other words, even before the plagues start, God tells Moshe that Pharaoh will ignore them. Nevertheless, God explains that He will bring them anyway so that Egypt shall *know* that He is God. This is not a matter of mere redemption or simple revelation. God could have lit up the sky with a flashing message or proclaimed His Existence in hundreds of other impressive ways. God is intent on providing Egypt, and hence the entire world, complete and unequivocal *knowledge* of His Existence — the type of knowledge hidden by the ten utterances of creation. Thus, it is not surprising to find that each of the ten plagues inversely corresponds to one of the ten utterances.

Rabbi Yehudah Loew of Prague, the Maharal (1525–1609), in his work *Gevuros Hashem*, Chapter 57, describes how each of the plagues corresponds to one of God's creation utterances. I also found this notion in the writings of Rabbi Gedalia Schorr (1910–1979) who was the Rosh Ha'yeshiva (Dean) of Mesivta Torah Vodaat in Brooklyn, New York, (*Ohr Gedalyahu, Moadim, pp. 138–142*) who focuses solely on the last three plagues and their relationship to the first three utterances.

The third utterance is as follows: "God said: 'Let there be a firmament in the midst of the waters, and let it separate between water and water'" (Gen. 1:6). On the first day God created the tangible existence, heaven and earth, but it was all undifferentiated. There was no division between spiritual and physical. In fact, there were no divisions at all. The only thing that existed was water. On day two, God separated the upper and lower waters. He created unique and distinct realms, thus establishing the framework for all of the specific details of the universe.

This concept is implicit in the eighth plague of *arbeh*, locusts. This word comes from the root *Resh-Bet-Heh* (Rabbah) meaning many, much, or a lot. There certainly were a lot of locusts. So many, in fact, that they completely covered the sur-

115

face of the land of Egypt and consumed any remaining vegetation. But the key connection here is this notion of "many." One cannot have many of something unless he owns less of something else or someone else owns less of that very thing. Without differentiation there can only be one. The fact of *arbeh*, as a concept, reveals the creative power hidden by the third utterance.

The second creation utterance is as follows: "And God said, 'Let there be light,' and there was light" (Gen. 1:3). The ninth plague was the Plague of Darkness. We can certainly see the symmetry between the creation of light and the withholding of light. However, the connection is even more direct than this. When the Torah describes the Plague of Darkness it first states the obvious, that the Egyptians could not see each other for the duration of the plague. However, it then adds another piece of information: "But for all the Children of Israel there was light in their dwellings" (Ex. 10:23). The miracle associated with this plague of darkness included the light for the Children of Israel. It may have been a plague of darkness, but it was a miracle of light, as well. This light was rather important for them, aside from the fact that it gave them the ability to function normally. With this light the Jews could find and identify the valuables of the Egyptians so that when they would finally leave they would be able to "borrow" them. This would enable God to fulfill his promise to Avraham that after the exile and slavery they would depart with a great treasure.

The final plague was the slaying of the firstborn: "I shall go through Egypt on this night and I shall strike every firstborn in the land of Egypt from man to beast: and against all gods of Egypt I shall mete out punishment — I am God" (Ex. 12:12).

As the Haggadah teaches in connection with this verse, God Himself — no angels or messengers or seraphs — redeemed the Jewish People and punished the Egyptians. With this final plague, God ended the game. Pharaoh not only conceded; he actually forced the Jews to leave. God fulfilled His commitment to the Children of Israel with this, the ultimate of plagues.

We previously discussed the nature of the first utterance, "bereishit," and the fact that it was qualitatively different from all others. There are several midrashim that link this first word to the relationship between the Jewish People and God.

Representative of these is *Vayikra Rabbah* 36:4:

> Rabbi Brechya states: "The heavens and earth were only created in the merit of Israel, as it says, 'In the beginning God created' (Genesis 1:1) and the term beginning or first (*reishit*) only refers to Israel as it says 'Israel is holiness unto God and the first fruits of his produce'" (Jeremiah 2:3)

Reishit is *first*, Israel is *first*, God strikes the *firstborn* of Egypt, in a measure for measure act, and through this penultimate action frees the Children of Israel and reveals Himself to all. This certainly accounts for the unveiling of the ten utterances.

Moshe describes this directly in Exodus 11:4 and 5: "And Moshe said, 'So said God, "at about midnight I shall go out in the midst of Egypt. Every firstborn in the land of Egypt shall die, from the firstborn of Pharaoh who sits on his throne to the firstborn of the maidservant...."'" The Targum Onkelos provides the real meaning of Verse 4. Rather than translating God's words literally — "I shall go out" — he uses a different phrase, *"Ani misgali bgo Mitzrayim"* (I will be *revealed* in the midst of Egypt). Just as God hid Himself through the ten utterances — from the beginning of Genesis where He was revealed clearly — so here, at the completion of the ten plagues, God stands fully revealed.

In summary, what we see from this comparison — how God hid His power in the layers of creation and revealed them to all during the exodus from Egypt — is a paradigm for how God interacts with the world. We should understand that all of creation — every life and every action — is a miracle. In the *Modim* prayer in the Amidah we thank God "for Your miracles that are with us every day; and for Your wonders and favors in every season — evening, morning, and afternoon." However, all of this miraculous activity is covered in nature, coincidence, and expectation. There was likely no process more miraculous than God's creation of the world. However, most scientists chase theories and patterns, rather than ascribing creation to God, because He hid all the miracles, and hence much of the evidence of His actions, within process.

This same comparison, God acting but hiding His actions, and God acting in an open and revealing way, also defines the relationship between Pesach and Purim. The exodus of the Jews from Egypt presents one miracle after another. The events are epic, even supernatural. In the Haggadah, the sages debate the number of miracles the people witnessed. When He freed the Jews from Egyptian bondage, God operated outside of human ability and comprehension.

Purim is an entirely different story. Here the fate of all of the Jews in the known world seems placed into the hands of the wicked Haman. God seems hidden and distant. The name of God does not directly appear even one time in the Book of Esther. So many events seem to line up just the right way: Esther becomes queen, Mordechai overhears a plot against the king, the king has a sleepless night and his squire just happens to read to him of the unrewarded loyalty of Mordechai; Haman just happens to be "hanging around" the palace as the king contemplates a reward for Mordechai, etc. It is all a matter of good fortune, politics, and coincidence. These are all natural forces operating.

Of course we know better. It is all the Hand of God. He directs every event, every action, and every reaction. However, rather than operating in an open and miraculous fashion, God is hiding in nature. This is the God of the ten utterances, not the God of the ten plagues. This is a case of redemption rather than salvation. So the question is:

What is the definition of redemption in this context?

I believe the answer is found in the very first discussion between God and Moshe concerning the exodus. God has just introduced Himself to Moshe, set out the problem (the Jews are being oppressed), and laid out the task for Moshe to go to Pharaoh and take the Children of Israel out of Egypt. Moshe, somewhat overwhelmed by this revelation, understandably reacts by asking who is he, to undertake and successfully complete such a fabulous and, in context, rather incredible mission. In Exodus 3:12, God gives Moshe the ultimate answer: "And He said, 'For I shall be with you — and this is your sign that I have sent you; When you take the people out of Egypt you will serve the people on this mountain.'"

If Moshe lacked confidence and sought assurance for the success of his mission, it would have sufficed for God to simply say, "you will succeed because I will be with you." But God elaborates, adding the "sign" that the mission will be deemed successful when they return to Sinai. Rashi comments, quoting the Midrash, that God is really defining the nature and purpose of the redemption. What God is saying is, "I have a great stake in this exodus, for in the future, Israel will receive the Torah about two months after departing Egypt." In fact, the expectation that they will receive the Torah is the catalyst for God's actions. In a sense God is extending them credit: He acts now, they pay later. Thus, the emancipation from slavery was just a step in the larger process. The true and complete redemption, as well as freedom and the responsibilities that come with it, is associated with receiving the Torah at Sinai. The exodus is the first step that enabled Israel to receive the Torah so it is called a *geula*, redemption.

If the redemption from Egypt was actually the act of accepting and receiving the Torah, then we should be able to find a similar redemption in the Purim story. However, in contrast with the Pesach-era acceptance, accompanied by the pyrotechnics and wonders at Sinai, we would expect to find a more subtle, natural acceptance in the Megillah.

The Book of Esther states: "The Jews confirmed and undertook upon themselves (*kimu ve'kiblu*) and their posterity and upon all those that join them, to observe these two days, without fail in the manner prescribed, and at the proper time each year" (Esther 9:27). This seems like a rather straightforward verse that explains that the Jews established Purim as an annual holiday. However, the Talmud reveals a far deeper meaning:

Rava said: "Even though Israel accepted the Torah, even so they accepted it again in the time of Achashveirosh, as it is written, 'They confirmed and undertook upon themselves (*kimu ve'kiblu*),' they confirmed that which they had already received" (*Shabbat* 88a).

We need a little background to fully appreciate Rava's comment. In the middle of the narrative relating the giving of the Torah at Sinai, we read that as Moshe brought the people forth to meet God, "[t]hey stood under the mountain" (Ex. 19:17). In the Talmud (also *Shabbat* 88a), Rav Avdima bar Chama explains that God held Sinai over them in a threatening manner. If they received the Torah, fine. If not, this spot would be their burial ground. This is in stark contrast to the image of the Jews answering, "We will do and we will listen (*na'aseh ve'nishma*)" in a manner that even astounded the angels. The Talmud goes on to explain that God actually performed a great service to the Jews by "compelling" their acceptance. He knew that in a mere forty days they would grievously sin by worshipping the Golden Calf. By holding the mountain over them, He provided them with a defense: "You cannot kill us for violating your covenant; we never willingly signed on. You compelled us, we did not accept willingly."

In the context of our previous discussion of the relationship between the ten utterances and the ten plagues, this explanation of the Talmud is right on the mark. We do not have to understand this story literally. Since at this juncture God had peeled back all of the layers obscuring clear knowledge of His existence and power, there really was no longer, for these people, such a thing as free choice. Their acceptance of the Torah was thus compelled rather than voluntary.

When the revelation is supernatural and when the events leading to it are supernatural, there is a supernatural redemption — but it is deemed forced; acceptance cannot be denied. However, Purim presented a different relationship with God — process, coincidence, and nature. If they chose to see and accept God's role in their redemption, as they did ("they confirmed and undertook upon themselves" [*kimu ve'kiblu*]), then the acceptance of the Torah logically followed afterward.

Of course, there is also an alternative explanation of the verse in Esther that defines the relationship between Sinai and Purim with a slightly different twist. At Sinai the Jews accepted only the written Torah but on Purim they accepted the oral Torah as well. This explanation fits within the framework of our discussion. Pesach and the experience of the Jews as they left Egypt was about what they saw and what God openly revealed. Purim involves the hidden, the subtle, the process of learning and deriving God's law rather than just receiving it on a silver platter.

Rabbi Boruch Halevi Epstein (1860–1920), in his work *Torah Temimah*, points out how closely the two acceptances of the Torah by the Jewish People parallel each other. At Sinai they proclaim, "We will do and we will listen (*na'aseh ve'nishma*)." God and the angels praised them for this because this acceptance runs counter to expected practice. Generally when a person is negotiating a contract or accepting responsibility, he wants to know what the terms are — he wants to listen and then accept. Here, they accepted blindly. In Esther, the structure of their response is the same — they confirmed and undertook upon themselves (*kimu ve'kiblu*). One would typically accept something before confirming it. However, they unconditionally confirmed their commitment to God and His Torah. The acceptance of Purim thus was nearly the same in every way, but for the spectacle of Sinai.

The events parallel and the redemptions parallel. One is natural and one is supernatural. At this point there should be no doubt that the concept of redemption relates to the receipt of Torah after leaving Egypt and later, when saved from the plot of Haman.

However, I believe that there is one more remarkable set of proofs establishing this understanding of redemption. God speaks to the Children of Israel in the first of the Ten Commandments by proclaiming and commanding: "I am the Lord, your God, Who has taken you out of the land of Egypt, from the house of slavery" (Ex. 19:2). As we asked at the outset, why does God not identify Himself as the Creator and Master of the Universe? Additionally, why is this the first time that God is making this declaration? Why did He not make this proclamation the night they left Egypt or right after the Egyptians drowned in the Red Sea?

In line with our understanding, remember that God is making this statement within the context of giving the Torah to Israel. If the redemption is defined, as we have discussed, as not merely leaving Egyptian bondage, but as freedom coupled with acceptance of the Torah, this is the very first moment when God can make this proclamation. Until He commenced transmitting the Torah, the redemption was not complete. This statement is, thus, not a statement of historical record or of God establishing His *bona fides*; it is a simple declaration that describes what is happening right then, at that precise moment. It may be true that God is the Creator and Master of the Universe, but that does not matter right now. What matters is that the commitment to the forefathers has been fulfilled. What matters now is that a relationship can now be built on trust because God has completed His task. Leaving Egypt did not matter and the death of the Egyptians did not matter. Sinai matters! The ten utterances and the ten plagues are completed with the Ten Commandments, with Torah.

If we turn back to Chapter 9 in the Book of Esther we find one last connection between Pesach and Purim. Actually it is more of a hint than a direct connection. Verses 10, 12, and 25, which precede the "confirmation and undertaking" in Verse 27, all reference the hanging of the sons of Haman. Haman, of course, had ten sons. Thus we make three references to ten in connection with Purim — a hint of the utterances, the plagues, and the commandments? Perhaps.

We now may also have an answer to the final question, why two and ten seem to reference the same thing in *Echad Mi Yode'a*? There were two acceptances of Torah — not just the first and second sets of tablets but the written and the oral, the visible and the studied. You can look at the magnificent tablets, carved by the Hand of God, and you can accept the Torah. However, for it to last you need to study the words and understand the Ten Commandments. Only then can you confirm.

Even these numbers — two and ten — and their relationship are not random in the context of this understanding. There are seven spaces between two and ten, like the seven weeks between Pesach and Shavuot. These holidays — Purim, Pesach, and Shavuot — are all connected to Jewish redemption.

In Chapter 1 we noted that there is a connection between the first night of Pesach and Tishah B'Av, a link between the ultimate redemption and the ultimate sign of exile. Among the lamentations that we recite on Tishah B'Av is a poem called *Aish Tukad Be'kirbi* ("A fire burns within me") that contrasts the sights, sounds, and wonders of the exodus from Egypt with those of the horrors of the exile from Yerushalayim. The last stanza, however, provides a message of hope: "Torah and testimony and the cherished vessels when I went forth from Egypt; gladness and joy, while anguish and sighing flee, when I return to Yerushalayim."

Perhaps when we learn to recognize the miracles that surround us every day through the medium of Torah, we will be able to answer the questions that will unleash the spectacular miracles of the final redemption.

• • • TESHUVAH BRINGS GEULA • • •

As I completed this chapter with the connection between these two periods of geula, I realized that the link between these holidays is further emphasized by four special Torah readings that we add on two Shabbatot before Purim and on two between Purim and Pesach (see *Mishana Megillah 3:4).* These portions, referred to as "The Four Portions" (*Arba'ah Parshiot)* are *Shekalim (*Ex. 30:11–17), which deals with the half-shekel that each adult male contributed both as a census and as a way of funding the annual communal offerings; *Zachor* (Deut. 25:17–19), which relates the command to remember Amalek's actions; *Parah* (Num. 19:1–22), which relates the laws of the red heifer; and *Chodesh* (Ex. 12:1–20), which contains the first mitzvah of establishing a calendar as well as the instructions given to the Jewish People as they prepared to leave Egypt.

The Rambam devotes an entire section of his *Mishne Torah* to the laws of repentance. In Chapter 2:2 he sets out the four steps or stages that are necessary for a complete teshuvah. These steps are: 1) regretting the sinful action (*charata*), 2) confessing the sin verbally (*vidduy*), 3) leaving the pattern of conduct (*azivat hachet*), and 4) accepting that one will never commit the sin again (*kabbalah al ha'atid*).

Are there parallels between the themes of the Four Portions and the Rambam's four stages of teshuvah?

Of the four stages of teshuvah, the only one that the Rambam identifies as a *mitzvah* is vidduy, confession. Why must we verbally confess? God knows our thoughts. He can certainly read our minds or simply understand if we just think our confessions. However, we are defined as human by our breath and our ability to speak. So, in order to receive atonement we must symbolically give these back to God. We must express with our words and spirit the depth of our folly. The mitzvah component is the one that effects the atonement.

In the reading for *Shekalim,* the Jewish People are likewise being asked to "give" something to God, a symbolic half-shekel. In a sense, this is almost silly. God is the Master of the entire universe. Why would He need a measly half-shekel? He certainly knows how many Jews there are without counting the coins. The answer is emphasized again and again in the reading. This is not a mere donation. It is "to atone for your souls" (Ex. 30:15), it is "the silver of atonement" (Ex. 30:16) and "a remembrance before God for the Children of Israel to atone for your souls" (Ex. 30:16). It is not just money or just a donation. Like the vidduy, it is something given to receive atonement.

In order to regret the sin you have to remember it. You need to remember the circumstances, the motivation. You will want to understand how the sin crept past your defenses. You will want to appreciate that things were not as good or did not work out as well as you thought they would. Only then can you feel the shame and the regret. The sin cannot be some abstract concept or some faraway act. The shame must burn within you.

That is similar to the emotion we associate with Amalek. When they attacked us after we crossed the Red Sea, preying on our weak and infirm, they epitomized evil — the type of evil that we must rid the world of. God did not want their actions to fade within our collective experience. God wanted, in fact commanded, us to remember everything about Amalek. The reading sets the scene for Amalek's action and details their shameful conduct. We must remember and regret our sins with the intensity of passion.

After confessing and regretting, we must leave the conduct. In other words, we must purify ourselves from the corruption and defilement. If we eat things that are not kosher, we have to stop. If we engage in illicit conduct, we must sever the relationships. If we waste our time in spiritually unhealthy activities, we must change our preferences and routines. We must change. We must shed the label of sinner and acquire the status of penitent!

The ashes of the red heifer symbolize this transformation. One minute a person is *tamei,* ritually impure, because he had to come into contact with a dead body. After undergoing the process (which involves being sprinkled with the ashes on the third and the seventh day) the person is transformed into one who is *tahor*, pure. Unfortunately, our process of self-improvement and teshuvah is not as simple or automatic; however, the end result is the same. As the Talmud, *Yoma* 85b, relates in the name of Rabbi Akiva: "You are praiseworthy O Israel, you have become purified before and are purified by your Father in heaven." When God accepts our teshuvah, we are purified, as if by the ashes of the red heifer or the waters of a *mikvah*.

The final step towards teshuvah is to accept in one's heart that he will not commit the sin again. God is actually rather generous here. The standard that we are held to is not the reality of our future conduct (which He knows right now and we do not); rather it is the sincerity of our belief at this moment of teshuvah. If you are sincere right now and not intending to commit this sin ever again, God will forgive you.

If there is one mitzvah that allows us — in fact, requires us — to look to the future, it is the establishment of the new month (*kiddush hachodesh*), the opening theme of the *Hachodesh* reading. First of all, by setting when a month starts, we establish the future, such as when the fifteenth is, and thus, perhaps, the day of a *yom tov* such as Succot or Pesach. Second, we do not set our calendar by the sun, which always appears with the same fullness. We use the moon. The moon grows, then recedes, and then grows again. We establish the month when it is nearly invisible, knowing that it will soon be full. Whatever it is today, it will be something different tomorrow. The moon represents change. We may be sinners today, but we can change and be righteous tomorrow.

The fact that these teshuvah themes overlay a period of geula may be an indication that God gives us multiple opportunities to do teshuvah each year because He wants us to hasten the coming of the Mashiach. Hopefully, one day we will collectively take advantage of the chances God gives us.

The "Good" Day

Lag B'Omer

• • • FRUIT PICKING • • •

A popular family activity is to pick fruit at the orchard. One orchard that we have frequented offers the customers the opportunity to pick raspberries, as well as apples. There is more skill and challenge involved in this. When you pick apples at an orchard, the helpers point you in the direction of a section where the fruit is ready, you stand beside the tree and you simply pick off the fruit. You might glance at the color or look to see if any portion of the apple is damaged, but each tree has may clusters of apples and you can fill your bag in practically no time at all.

Raspberries are another story, altogether. You could spend a half-hour walking up and down the rows of bushes locating and picking the berries to fill just two small containers. On any given bush at the orchard, you might find one or two berries that are ripe enough for picking. You have to look all over the bush, avoid thorns, lift branches, and when you finally find one or two that are ready, you must gently but firmly pull the fruit away from the stem. Sometimes one large bush may yield only one small berry. So you move on to the next and the next, all the way down the row. As you get to the end of the row, you might well glance back in the direction from which you had just picked. The splashes of red color from the bushes that you thought had no more berries catch your eye and cause you to pause.

It seems that while moving forward in one direction with a certain perspective, we see certain things. We see them clearly and act. However, with a change of position and focus we realize how much more there was to see. How could we have missed all of those berries? Where were they when we examined each bush closely, when we lifted and pulled? Look how many beautiful ripe raspberries we can still harvest from the very bush that we would have sworn had no more to give!

The process of studying Torah is likened to an orchard. In fact, the major methods of study are described using the mnemonic *Peh, Resh, Daled, Samech* — *pardes* — which stands for *Peshat* (literal textual meaning), *Remez* (textual hints and references), *Drash* (exegesis and investigation), and *Sod* (secrets, *Kabbalah*). The word *pardes* in Hebrew means orchard. One of the most mysterious passages in the Talmud, *Chagiga* 14b, involves the four great sages, Rabbi Akiva, Ben Zoma, Ben Azzai, and Elisha ben Avuya, who entered the *pardes* to undertake a detailed examination of the secrets of the process of creation. Only one, Rabbi Akiva, came out intact. Of the others, one died, one went insane, and one abandoned Judaism and became a heretic. Pardes, thus, can be dangerous. However, if one receives proper guidance, one can learn to see many new things in the Torah and to learn about the depth of many of the special days in the cycle of our year.

Few, if any, today are experts in this type of analysis. However, pardes seemed to be the province of several masters of *chassidut*. One such master was Rabbi Tzvi Elimelech Shapiro of Dinov (1783–1841), called Bnei Yissas'char, for the best known of his works. This book presents the months of the year and their special days and character through a kabalistic perspective. Let us experience a taste of the Torah from the pardes of the Bnei Yissas'char through his analysis of the day known as *Lag B'Omer.*

Lag B'Omer (the eighteenth day of Iyar), is the thirty-third of the forty-nine days that we count from the second day of Pesach until Shavuot. This period was originally a happy time, a time to prepare spiritually for receiving the Torah and for refining ourselves spiritually. In fact, the two harvests for this time period in Israel, the barley harvest and the wheat harvest, provide a metaphor for this process of self-improvement. On the second day of Pesach, the kohen brought the omer offering, a measure of barley — a coarse grain fit for consumption by animals. After the Jewish Nation progressed through the next seven weeks to the time of the wheat harvest, the kohen on Shavuot brought the offering of the two loaves — bread made of wheat, the food of man. Each year, we thus symbolically advance from the coarseness of barley to the refinement of wheat.

In the period of Roman domination following the destruction of the Second Temple, the omer period became associated with mourning and sorrow. During this time, in some type of plague, massacre, or other calamity, twenty-four thousand students of Rabbi Akiva died. There are different traditions concerning which days are associated with the deaths. However, we identify the thirty-third day as one which the deaths either stopped altogether or, at the very least, paused. While we know that it is a special day, a day that was not touched by sorrow, we do not know why this is so. The analysis of the Bnei Yissas'char provides an understanding into this mystery.

Additionally, this day is identified as the *yom hilula* (the day of memorial rejoicing) for Rabbi Shimon bar Yochai. Many sources identify him as the author of the *Zohar*, the major work of Jewish mysticism, which is primarily a Midrash commentary on the written Torah. The *Zohar* provided the foundation for the later study of Kabbalah by the Lurianic School, and thus strongly influenced the development and growth of chassidut. Accordingly, this makes Lag B'Omer a fitting subject for applying the methods and insights that evolved from Rabbi Shimon bar Yochai's own teachings.

• • • THE GOLDEN RULE • • •

One of the greatest leaders and teachers in Jewish tradition was the sage Rabbi Yochanan ben Zakkai. He lived during the time frame of the destruction of the Second Temple. In fact, as related in the Talmud, *Gittin* 56a–b, he was responsible for the fact that the sages survived and were allowed to establish a religious haven in the city of Yavne — he negotiated with the Roman general Vespasian who had been sent by the emperor to destroy Yerushalayim. He was a student of and successor to the great Hillel. He, in turn, left behind five illustrious students: Rabbi Eliezer ben Hyrkanos, Rabbi Yehoshua ben Chanania, Rabbi Yose the Kohen, Rabbi Shimon ben Netanel, and Rabbi

Elazar ben Arach (*Pirkei Avot,* 2:10).

The Mishnah, *Pirkei Avot* 2:13, relates a discussion that Rabbi Yochanan had with his five students:

> He said to them: "Go out and see what is the proper way to which a man should cling ['The Golden Rule']." Rabbi Eliezer says: "A good eye." Rabbi Yehoshua says: "A good friend." Rabbi Yose says: "A good neighbor." Rabbi Shimon says: "One who considers the outcome of a deed." Rabbi Elazar says: "A good heart." He [Rabbi Yochanan] said to them: "I prefer the words of Elazar ben Arach to your words, for your words are included in his."

This discussion raises far more questions than it seems to answer.

- If the greatest rabbi of a generation asks his students what is most important in life, would you not expect them to propose answers like "the Torah," "following God's commandments," "having unwavering faith in God," or any of a number of other fundamentals of our faith? What are these good eye, good friends, and good neighbor responses? This seems more like a commercial for insurance rather than a crucial theological discussion.

- Before asking the question, Rabbi Yochanan implores them to "go out and see." What does he want them to look at? Are they providing observations or a thought process?

- Where do these answers come from? These sages had an encyclopedic knowledge of the written and oral Torah. If their teacher were asking a question this important, one would surmise that they were not just answering flippantly, off the top of their heads. They would most likely be basing their positions on a tradition or a textual source. If so, which sources?

• Finally, after they all answer, Rabbi Yochanan comments that the other four answers are included within that of Rabbi Elazar, "a good heart." How do we derive the other concepts from this one?

In order to answer these questions, the Bnei Yissas'char starts by using a concept that can be described as "first use." First use, in the realm of Kabbalah and biblical exegesis is the first time that a word or letter or name or concept appears in the Torah. That first use, in context, itself becomes a part of the definition that carries forward throughout the Torah. Think of how the first man Adam is the template and paradigm for all men. In much the same way, many other firsts in the Torah represent other more timeless themes.

The Talmud in *Bava Kama* 55a teaches, "If one sees the [Hebrew] letter *tet* in a dream, this is a good omen — since the first time that the Torah employs the letter tet is within the word "good" (tov, *tet-vav-vet*). Thus, since the first use of the tet is for good, this letter represents good. Let us linger on this word tov, for a moment. Tov, besides meaning good, is also used to describe the Torah, as the verse in *Mishle* 4:2, states: "For I have given you a good ("tov") teaching, do not forsake my Torah." The Midrash in fact states, there is no good ("tov") except Torah.

The Bnei Yissas'char informs us that these sages are clearly not pulling answers out of the air. In fact, they are doing exactly what their teacher instructed them to do — to

"Go out and see!" What are they looking at? They are looking at the ultimate source, in Torah, of course. Like the rabbis who ventured into the pardes, they were being provided with direction for examining the very beginning of the Torah, the most mystical and crucial of all its portions.

Look at the question that Rabbi Yochanan asks at the start of this perhaps ultimate lesson. He is not asking about the "proper path" (*derech yesharah*), he is asking about the "good path" (*derech tovah*). (In fact, the second chapter of *Pirkei Avot* begins with a definition of derech yesharah, provided by Rabbi Yehuda the Prince — who compiled the Mishnah — that bears no relationship to these answers.) Note the precise focus of his question, "The *good* way." He is teaching a lesson in the *tov* of creation.

Immediately from the first response, that of Rabbi Eliezer, we see that his students knew what Rabbi Yochanan was looking for. As Rabbi Eliezer answers, "A good eye [ayin tov]," he immediately places the focus on good. But his answer, like the question, is much deeper than that. The answer reveals both source and reason. Look carefully at the first use of tov in the Torah. "And God saw that the light was good ..." (Genesis 1:4). The first time good is used is in connection with God seeing the light. God's seeing was good. Another way to express this, since humans associate sight with the eye, is to say, as Rabbi Eliezer did, ayin (eye) tov (good).

Rabbi Yehoshua, likewise, understood the question within this context. He, too, looked at the opening verses of our Torah and the relationship between what God was doing and the first use of tov. After the initial creation of heaven and earth, there is only darkness: "with darkness upon the surface of the deep ..." (Gen. 1:2). God then creates light. However, that light is intermingled with the dark. They are indistinguishable, a fusion of light and dark. The Hebrew word for connection or fusion is *chibbur (chet-bet-resh)*. It is also the root of the word for friend, *chaver (chet-bet-resh)*. Thus, when God looks at the light and says that it is good, He is actually, at least according to Rabbi Yehoshua, commenting on the goodness of the cojoined entities of light and dark — otherwise expressed as "chaver tov (good friend)."

Rabbi Yose views these same events, but he believes that you need to go a little further in the text in order to fully understand the context. Yes, there was dark, followed by the creation of light, which resulted in a fusion. However, Rabbi Yose implores us to look at the full verse. "And God saw the light was good, and God *separated* (vayavdel) between the light and the darkness" (Gen. 1:4). According to Rabbi Yose, it was not the initial creation of light and dark that was "good." If this were so, God would not have immediately acted to change it. The real good was the fact that when separated, the two entities of light and dark could take complementary roles. One would define day and one would define night. Without the other, neither had independent significance, as they could not be a reference point for the passage of time. What was good was not the fusion but the cooperation. They were separate, but interdependent — like good neighbors — *shachen (shin-chaf-nun)*, hence, shachen (*shin-chaf-nun*) tov.

This concept of shachen, which we have been translating as neighbor, is actually much more complex. It represents co-existence that goes far beyond just physical proximity. It often describes a transcendental state where two opposites can both assert their essence. A great example of this is the Tabernacle (Mishkan, mem-shin-chaf-nun) and the Temples. God refers to these collectively as the "place that the Lord, your God, will choose to rest His Name" (Deut. 16:11). On the one hand we have God, Who is non-corporeal in all respects. His Name is representative of power and prayer and spirit that cannot be structured. Yet, this Name will be contained in a place. What a contradiction. Yet God allows this *shikkun*, this coexistence, much the way He allows light and dark to coexist, in the state we call twilight.

Rabbi Shimon takes a slightly different approach. Thematically, he is in the same text, and he focuses on the same word, tov, but his perspective is influenced by even more mystical goings-on. We have quoted Genesis 1:4 several times and have already discussed it within three other contexts, but we have examined the baseline explanation. For this we turn to Rashi who writes:

> "And God saw that the light was good and He sep-arated." For this too we need to use the words of the Agaddah. He saw that it was not proper for the wicked to use this light and He separated it for the righteous for the days to come. (*Chagiga* 12a).

There are a few things bothering Rashi in this verse. First, if the light is "good," why does God immediately separate it? Second, if the sun, moon, and stars are not created until day four, what is the nature of this light and where is it now? Rashi turns to the Midrash to explain that the original light was something spiritual and special rather than a mere source of illumination. In fact, God determined that this light was so good that He decided that He did not want to share it with wicked people, who would eventually live in this world. Instead, He placed in it in storage for the righteous in the future. Accordingly, He created other sources of illumination for the necessary light of this world on the fourth day.

Rabbi Shimon's answer, that the good path is a function of being "one who considers the outcome of a deed," thus relates to how God acted with regard to the creation of light. God understood the nature of the light and then considered its use in the future. The verse juxtaposes "good" with "and He separated" to highlight that this sequence represents: 1) taking consideration of the future, and 2) acting in accordance with this consideration — which for Rabbi Shimon represents this first Divine "good."

Now we are ready for the correct answer, the one that Rabbi Yochanan said includes all of the others. Rabbi Elazar's answer is at once the most simple and the deepest. He says that the good way is "lev tov" (a good heart). If we look in these verses we see no hearts; in fact, there are no living things. There are no emotions, the province of the heart. So what/where is Rabbi Elazar's heart?

Once again the Bnei Yissas'char explains this by moving our frame of reference — showing us those raspberries on the other side of the bush. Do not focus on lev as heart. Instead move back to that tov. We know tov is the key to it all. Count the words until you reach that first tov. There are thirty-two words until that tov. The word for heart, lev, is spelled lamed-vet. The numerical equivalent, or gematria, of this word is thirty-two. Lev tov is not a concept; it is a map. Rabbi Elazar is being profoundly literal. The path to tov is past the first thirty-two words of the Torah. After thirty-two words the light of the Torah begins to shine. That is the light that is good, the light of the Torah!

Of course, that begs the question of just what this light is. This answer can also be found within the words themselves. Literally, the object that God declares good is "the light" (*et ha'or*). These two words are spelled *aleph-tav, heh-aleph-vav-resh*. The numerical values of these letters are 1+400+5+1+6+200 = 613, as in the six hundred and thirteen mitzvot. Rabbi Elazar's answer absolutely includes all the others. His answer, so deep and yet so simple, for defining the "good way" is Torah. Everything else, as they say, is just commentary and explanation.

But we cannot stop there. We need to apply this to the Torah of the ages, our Torah and our experience as God's Chosen People. In other words, this math lesson is not quite over. We already discussed that lev is thirty-two. But there is another part of Rabbi Elazar's map. The original map led to the first tov, so we stopped there. However, we do not just stop at the beginning; we move through history. If we do not stop after lev, we must consider the tov. The word tov is spelled *tet-vav-bet*. The numerical value of these letters is 9+6+2 = 17. If we add seventeen to thirty two, the result is … forty-nine. Rabbi Elazar certainly knows the significance of this number. There are forty-nine stages of preparation to receive the Torah. The Children of Israel ascended one level each day after leaving Egypt until finally, on the sixth of Sivan, on Shavuot, they were ready for the Torah.

However, Rabbi Elazar also knows that these forty-nine days are like the first lev tov. First, there is the passing of thirty-two, *lev*, and then the *or*, the spiritual light of Torah (which is

140

tov), is revealed. The day first associated with this light cannot be a day of sorrow, mourning, or plague. Lag B'Omer must thus be an oasis — a day when tragedy stops and on which there must be an element of joy. Likewise, it is so fitting that the day is later associated with Rabbi Shimon bar Yochai, who wrote the *Zohar*, a word that itself means light or illumination.

In Psalms 119:18, King David writes: "Open my eyes that I may behold wondrous things from Your Torah." The word David chooses for opening his eyes is *gal* (*gimel-lamed*), which is usually translated as 'to reveal.' David could have chosen a form of *liftoach* (*peh-tav-chet, patach*) — opening or *lifkoach* (*peh-kuf-chet, pakach*) — comprehending. Why did he choose this particular verb? The answer, in part, turns on this word's gematria. We can convert *gimel* and *lamed* into 3+30, which is our same thirty-three. David associates the revelation of Torah, or more accurately, the ability to glance from a distance and see the Torah with thirty-three. Lag B'Omer is the day that affords us that first glance of the holy spiritual light of Torah. May we merit the time when this light of Torah will shine brightly on all of our days.

CHAPTER

8

The Twenty-Two Days of Summer

The Three Weeks and the Month of Elul

• • • BALANCE • • •

A few years ago a local radio station ran a promotion it called the "Ninety-One Days of Summer." Each day that summer it sponsored some grand event — a concert, a beach party, a picnic, a boat ride, etc. The station ran many ads in the newspaper, purchased space on prominent billboards, and found many other clever ways to promote its own promotion. The tone of the campaign was that since the summer is a time for fun, fun, and more fun, the station wanted to be the official sponsor of that fun — and presumably it hoped people would then listen to the station because it enabled this gaiety.

When I thought about this promotion, it occurred to me that for most of the world there is something about the summer that implies fun. Likely the combination of relaxed schedules (especially for students) and nice weather create a mood that motivates people to want to go out and do things — to engage in recreation, entertainment, and amusements. In contrast, if you look at the Jewish calendar during these months (late June through late September) you encounter two of the most serious times of the year. In July–August we experience the Three Weeks, which are bracketed by the Seventeenth of Tammuz and the Ninth of Av. These weeks are the most profoundly mournful of the entire year. Three weeks later (August into September) we enter the month of Elul. On Rosh Chodesh Elul we begin to blow the shofar each morning as a reminder that the Days of Awe are quickly approaching and that it is time to turn our full attention to teshuvah. In some years we celebrate Rosh Hashanah and Yom Kippur while it is still summer on the calendar of seasons. Thus while society around us is immersed in revelry, we must focus our thoughts and actions on spirituality and elevation.

The contrast is almost shocking: while summer is, for some, a period of endless parties, for us it is a time of constraint and reflection. I believe there is a great lesson here in balance. If every day is a party, if life has no ups or downs, but just rolls on in endless celebration, where is personal growth? How will a person engaged in such constant pursuit of celebration adapt and handle adversity?

Judaism recognizes extremes of joy and sorrow. Perhaps the two best examples of these extremes of emotion are the celebration of a marriage and the mourning after the death of a loved one. Both life-cycle events — one incredibly joyous and the other incredibly sad — are marked by seven days of extremity. For the bride and groom the first seven days of their marriage is marked by daily parties in celebration of their union. For mourners, there are the seven days of shiva that are meant to help the family focus on and deal with their grief. Our religion provides circumscribed periods of intense experiences for both events. There is also a status of joy for the marriage that extends for a full year, just as there is an extension of certain mourning observances for a year — again the balance. But the most intense aspects of the celebration and the mourning run for the first week.

These two extremes illustrate the role of emotional and psychological balance within Judaism. There are times to rise way up, to celebrate and to revel. Likewise there are times to cry and to mourn and to feel depressed. But both of these extremes must have limits — or the ups and downs lose their meaning and we lose our self-identities. Ninety-one days of partying is not an endless summer; it is a bottomless emotional pit.

• • • THE THREE WEEKS— • • •
THE NARROW STRAITS

We have previously discussed each of the fast days and placed them in context. However, in order to better understand the period of the Three Weeks, we will briefly revisit the two most infamous of these days, Shiva Asar B'Tammuz and Tishah B'Av, and their source in the Mishnah as well as the source for some of the observances that surround these days:

> Five tragedies befell our fathers on the seventeenth of Tammuz and five on the ninth day of Av. On the seventeenth of Tammuz, the tablets were broken, the *tamid* was discontinued, the city was breached, Apustumus burned the Torah, and an idol was placed in the Sanctuary. On the ninth of Av, God decreed that our fathers would not enter the Land of

Israel, the First and Second Temples were destroyed, Beitar fell, and the city was plowed over. When the month of Av enters, we diminish our joy.

During the week in which the ninth of Av falls it is forbidden to cut one's hair or to wash one's clothes, but it is permitted on Thursday in honor of the Shabbat. On the eve of the ninth of Av one should not partake in two cooked dishes, nor should one eat meat or drink wine. Rabban Shimon ben Gamliel says, one should make some variation (i.e., change one's lifestyle to reflect the solemnity). Rabbi Yehuda required turning over the bed but the Rabbis did not agree with him (*Taanit* 4; 10 and 11).

What we learn from this is that while the two fasts are identified, the period of mourning or commemoration begins with the month of Av, with other observances for the week of the ninth, the eve of the ninth, and although not set out in this Mishnah, on the ninth itself.

However, in Jewish legal practice we find a variation on this, really more of an extension, that is linked with a phrase used in *Eichah* (The Book of Lamentations). The prophet laments: "Yehuda has gone into exile because of suffering and harsh toil. She dwelt among the nations but found no rest; all her pursuers overtook her between the straits (*bein hametzarim*)" (Lamentations 1:3). The Midrash (*Eichah Rabbah* 1:29) explains that the term "narrow straits" is a metaphor that refers to the three week time period that extends from Shivah Asar B'Tammuz to Tishah B'Av.

Accordingly, in Jewish Law we layer a variety of mourning practices, with increasing intensity as we approach Tishah B'Av.

••• JEWISH MOURNING AND ••• THE THREE WEEKS

Mourning is an important theme in Judaism, and it is particularly important to individual Jews. It is an opportunity for reflection and the means to achieve spiritual, emotional, and psychological healing. Throughout the book of Genesis, we witness death and the passing of generations. We learn how important proper burial is when Avraham negotiates a proper burial place for Sarah, as well as eulogizing her and crying over her loss (Gen. 23:2). We comprehend the importance of immediate burial when Yaacov buries Rachel in Bet Lechem, rather than transporting her body to Chevron (Gen. 35:19). And we witness the reuniting of Yaacov and Esav at the burial of Yitzchak (Gen. 35: 29). We do not encounter mourning practices themselves until the death of Yaacov.

When Yaacov died in Egypt, the Torah relates that the Egyptians mourned him in an extreme and elaborate way: "And they completed him for forty days, as such were the days of the embalmers. And Egypt cried for seventy days" (Gen. 50:3). In contrast, the Torah relates that when his sons transported him for burial, "and they intensely eulogized and he made for his father a seven-day mourning period" (Gen. 50:10). Could it be that the people of Egypt admired, loved, or respected Yaacov more than his own sons? They mourned ten times longer! However, for them it was unrestrained, extreme, undifferentiated — like that endless summer party. For the sons of Yaacov, for the Jewish People, there are limits, balance and sincere meaning. This is the source for the basic seven-day mourning period.

In Jewish law, we actually find six stages of mourning practice in the year after the death of a parent. From the moment of death until burial the mourner is an *onen*. His or her priority is to make the necessary preparations and arrangements for the funeral. This includes preparing the body, securing and preparing a burial plot, composing a eulogy, etc. Such a person is exempt from virtually all positive commandments — and may not pray, study Torah, don *tefillin* (phylacteries), etc. We do not comfort mourners before the funeral, although we can certainly offer assistance.

The second stage is the burial, the onset of mourning. After the burial, the bereaved are now called *aveilim*, mourners. All of the restrictions that apply to mourners now apply in full force — including not shaving or bathing, not wearing freshly laundered clothes, sitting on the floor or at a lower-than-normal level, etc. The third period is the first three days when the grief is at its peak. Some even have the custom not to visit the mourner during these days. A mourner may not be greeted during these first three days since he or she may not return the greeting. Fourth is the completion of shiva, days three to seven, when the edge is off slightly, when we have regular visitation, according to all customs, and when the mourner may extend a greeting. From day seven to day thirty is the fifth stage, a period called *shloshim* (literally, thirty). The mourner rises from the shiva period and reenters the world — returns to work and daily activities. While some of the mourning practices end with the shiva, others (like not cutting hair) continue for the first thirty days. Finally, there is the sixth stage, the extension from day thirty until the end of the first year — where there are a number of remaining restrictions, including not attending certain public entertainment performances or social gatherings.

These stages of mourning diminish in intensity and restriction to reflect the lessening of the grief and the healing passage of time. When we are more depressed we need more time to reflect and less activity. As we regain emotional balance, we move toward normal activity and interaction.

So, too, during the Three Weeks, we move through six stages or levels of restriction. However, these, with the exception of the last, increase in intensity and restriction rather than diminish:

In the first stage, beginning with Shivah Asar B'Tammuz and running until Rosh Chodesh Av, we curtail a number of pleasurable activities — no swimming, public (musical) entertainment, weddings, or hair cutting. We likewise avoid activities that would occasion our reciting the blessing of *Shehecheyanu,* which praises God, "Who has kept us alive, sustained us, and brought us into this season." Since this season of the Three Weeks is not particularly auspicious, we try to avoid reciting the blessing. Thus we do not wear new clothes, purchase new homes, eat new fruits, or do anything that would trigger the blessing.

The second stage commences with Rosh Chodesh Av (the beginning of a period termed The Nine Days) and includes additional restrictions including avoiding eating meat and drinking wine (except for Shabbat) and not wearing clean (i.e., freshly laundered) clothes. The third stage is called *Shavua Sh'Chal Bo* (the week in which Tishah B'Av falls). During this week we may not launder clothes or bathe our bodies. Fourth is the eve of Tishah B'Av. At this time we consume a special meal called a *seuda hamafseket* (the meal that marks a break between the time leading to Tishah B'Av and Tishah B'Av itself). At this meal we are not to consume a combination of two cooked foods and we are not to eat together with other people so as to create a social gathering for the purposes of the Grace After Meals.

The fifth stage is the most intense: Tishah B'Av. On this day we have all of the restrictions not of mere mourning, but the very afflictions Yom Kippur. We cannot eat or drink, wear leather shoes, wash any part of our bodies (except part of the hand when required for ritual washing), use fragrant oil, or engage in marital relations. In addition, for the first half of the day we observe some of the very customs of the mourner in shiva, including sitting on the ground or on low seats and not greeting people. Finally, there is the sixth stage, the Tenth of Av, where we return to the restrictions of the nine days until midday.

With this foundation in place, there are a number of questions that we must explore:

- Why is the mourning of the Three Weeks reversed from regular experience? In life we are shocked by loss and then slowly and methodically return to a point of balance. During the Three Weeks the intensity of mourning builds and there does not seem to be a release — certainly not a gradual release.
- Judaism infuses numbers with great significance. Sevens show up everywhere — the Shabbat, the length of holidays, mourning and weddings, the *shemitta* agricultural

cycle, and on and on. The numbers thirty, thirty-two, thirty-three, forty, forty-nine, and fifty all lead to multiple ideas. But where do we find twenty-one or twenty-two? Why do those numbers show up here in the Three Weeks?

- What is the Tenth of Av and what role does it play in moving beyond the three weeks?

- Where is the healing? Where is the cure? It seems like we reach this depth of sorrow, we experience the exile and the tragedy, we cry and recite elegies, and then...we just return to normal. This does not fit within normal experience and certainly not patterns of religious practice.

- Does this concept of six stages show up elsewhere in our year?

• • • AN EXAMPLE OF NON-MOURNING • • •

Earlier, when we reached back into the Book of Genesis to examine the source of mourning, we did not discuss one particular incident. This was an intentional omission, but not because I wanted to pull it out later, like a rabbit out of my hat, as a key to answering some of our questions. We did not discuss it because rather than being an example of mourning, the incident in question was actuality a case of non-mourning.

After Yosef's brothers sold him to the Ishmaelite caravan, they realized that they needed to cover up their crime. They slaughtered a goat and dipped Yosef's coat (the famed coat of many colors) into the blood. When they returned to Yaacov without Yosef and with the blood-soaked coat, the brothers did not have to tell any tales. They merely showed him the coat and allowed him to conclude, "a savage beast consumed him; Yosef has been torn to pieces" (Gen. 37:33). The brothers, of course, did nothing to disabuse this mistaken notion, since this is exactly what they wanted him to conclude. They were not going to lie to their father, but they did not mind that he drew a wrong conclusion and never asked them the direct question — what happened to Yosef?

Yaacov first reacts in an expected manner for a mourner; he rents his clothes, he dons sackcloth, "and he mourns over his son for many days" (Gen. 37:34). Then the Torah describes a rather peculiar behavior: "All his sons and daughters rose to console him, but he refused to be comforted and he said, 'I will go down to my grave mourning my son' (Gen. 37:35). Even at the outset, something inside of Yaacov recognizes that he will never accept Yosef's death. This seems rather extreme, especially for a man of Yaacov's stature and accomplishment, who has experienced all that he has in life, and who has eleven other sons. This is a man who is balanced, who has faced adversity and challenge. Why is he reacting this way?

Rashi on this verse answers: "A person will not receive consolation on a living person, even though the person is presumed dead." He then adds, quoting the Midrash and the Talmud, "Concerning a dead person a decree has been passed that he will be forgotten, not so however with a living person." The ability for a person to move on emotionally and psychologically after the death of a loved one is not a given. To the contrary, based on the way the human mind and memory function the pain would be constant and debilitating. However God presents the mourner with a gift — the ability to forget. Not to forget the person entirely, of course, but for the essence and importance of the deceased to the survivor to recede from active consciousness. God does not do this at once, like excising or amputating a limb from the body. Rather the memory fades during the course of the mourning process. By the time the year ends, there is still pain, but by then, usually, life can go on for the living as normal.

However, this rule only applies when the proper condition exists for its operation. God allows this decree of forgetfulness to apply only when the object is actually dead. If not, the grief is never-ending, as Yaacov experiences with Yosef. Yaacov cannot be consoled; the intensity of the emotional grief cannot fade because Yosef is still alive. Yaacov does not know or even suspect that Yosef lives. Based on the objective evidence it is his own belief that Yosef was devoured by a wild beast. Nevertheless, Yaacov's psyche, which is so in tune with his spirit, is completely restless and inconsolable. If the person or object being mourned is not truly lost, then there is no consolation.

The Ninth of Av, tracing back to the sin of the spies, is a day of "crying for the generations." It is an appropriate time to commemorate the destruction of the Temples, as it is the proper time to mourn the millions of Jews slaughtered in inquisitions, crusades, pogroms, and the Holocaust. But even on the afternoon of that very day, we begin to lighten the intensity of the mourning — we rise from our seats on the ground, we return to a level of daily activity. This seems strange; after all, the afternoon and even the next day were the prime hours of destruction. Things did not ease up that afternoon; they literally got worse. But we do not mourn this, or more accurately we do not confine our mourning because it is not natural. We mourn for the Temple every day. Our prayers are filled with longing for the return to Zion and for the restoration of the Temple service. During the week we preface the Grace After Meals with Psalm 137 — "If I forget thee O' Yerushalayim, let my right hand forget its skill." We do not forget, we do not allow the mourning to diminish, for even one day. We do not need to mourn on the tenth because we mourn on the eleventh, twelfth, thirteenth, etc., as well. Just as Yosef was really alive, we can still access the true power of the Temple service though the Temple itself appears to be lost.

The Jewish People ultimately survived the destruction of the Temple because they never lost the Temple's power. Their verbal recitation of the offerings at the appropriate times, "letting our lips compensate for the bulls" (*Hoshe'a* 14:3), would replace their physical Temple service. As we look at the portion detailing the daily offerings set out in the portion of Pinchat (Num. 28:1–39) we can count them as follows: The daily *Tamid* (1), the Musaf for Shabbat (1), the Musaf for Rosh Chodesh (1), the Musaf offerings for each day of Pesach (7), the Musaf for Shavuot (1), the Musaf for Rosh Hashanah (1), the Musaf for Yom Kippur (1), the Musaf for Succot (7), and the Musaf for Shemini Atzeret (1). Adding these up, we have twenty-one offerings that we no longer bring in the Temple, but that we incorporate into our prayers. These prayers protect us the same way the offerings themselves did. We have moved from physical to verbal offerings, external symbols to internal words. Three weeks are twenty-one days leading to Tishah B'Av. The mourning of that twenty-second day may be necessary, but it is not really natural. We have lost much, but we have not lost as much as we think we have!

The Temple would be transformed from an external location of spiritual power to an internal one. It is interesting
to note that this concept was implicit in the very command
that God gave the Children of Israel when He introduced the
concept of a constructed dwelling. "They shall make for Me a
sanctuary so that I may dwell in *them*" (Ex. 25:8). God does not
say that He may dwell within *it* but within *them*. The power
was always within the people, not within the building.

Yet we do have that twenty-second day and we do mourn
on Tishah B'Av. This mourning of twenty-two days is thus
a parallel to the unnecessary mourning that Yaacov did for
twenty-two years over Yosef!

But there is still one more message of twenty-two associated with these days: the message of balance. The ultimate
joy of marriage is contained within the same boundary as the
despair of loss. If we mourn for twenty-two days because of the
exile, God must balance it out with twenty-two days of joy, real
yom tov! In the exile, because of the extra day that is added
to each holiday other than Yom Kippur, we celebrate twenty-
two days of holiday, as follows: Pesach **(8)**, Shavuot **(2)**, Rosh
Hashanah **(2)**, Yom Kippur **(1)**, Succot **(8)**, Shemini Atzeret/
Simchat Torah **(1)**.

We now can comprehend some of the emotional and psychological issues of the Three Weeks. There is a balance in our
lives between joy and sadness. Both have their limits, lest we
fall prey to unnatural and unhealthy behavior. Similarly, even
when responding appropriately, with celebration or mourning, there is a logical progression — a waning of intensity as
the catalyst recedes into the past. When this pattern is not followed, we may assume that the underlying assumption is in-

accurate, the joy may have been an illusion, or as we have discussed, the loss is merely a failure to search within ourselves. Nevertheless, there always is a process, a series of rituals, levels, and observances. Why then do these Three Weeks seem to end so abruptly? We cry, we seek answers, and we want consolation. Yet after the ninth (or at most, midday on the tenth) everything goes back to normal immediately. Or does it?

• • • MOTION SICKNESS • • •

The Three Weeks ended rather abruptly, leaving in their wake unanswered questions and emptiness. We mourn the destruction of the Temples and the slaughter of countless Jewish martyrs throughout history. We cry through the murder and torture of ten of the greatest sages in history and are touched by the tragedy of the story of the son and daughter of Rabbi Yishmael the Kohen Gadol (High Priest). Then in short order we stand, shave, clean up, and go back to eating what we want and enjoying life the way we want.

This is like driving with someone who has a lead foot. Such a person accelerates rapidly at every green light, swerves into any traffic opening that may be moving a little more rapidly, and is constantly slamming the brakes rather than decelerating smoothly. This ride, with its abrupt stops and starts, is very discomforting to the passenger and often results in nausea and dizziness. However, the driver, although experiencing the same physical motions and forces, does not seem adversely affected. It may be that since the driver is controlling the movements of the vehicle and is deciding (consciously or subconsciously) the when and how, he is able to subtly shift and move, tense and relax his own body to minimize the extremes of the forces. The passenger, however, is merely being tossed to and fro, which exerts pressure on the body in a more extreme manner. At the end of the ride, upon reaching the destination, the driver may vigorously bound out of the car, while the passenger staggers out like a person shaking off a hangover.

Fundamentally, what is the difference here? They both sat in the same car, drove the same route, at the same speeds, with the same twists and turns. However one was somewhat in control and could see where he was heading, while the other could not. Our drive through the Three Weeks is a similar experience. If we understand where we have been and, more importantly, can anticipate what is just ahead, we can bound out, with seeming abruptness. If we cannot, then we stagger in a state of emotional turmoil.

• • • AHEAD AND BEHIND • • •

As we get out for a rest stop (perhaps a better analogy would be a scenic overlook) on midday on the Tenth of Av, we can choose to look forward or backward. If we look backward we see the six stages of mourning that are bracketed by Shiva Asar B'Tammuz and Tishah B'Av. As we look ahead, to the next important unit in our year… we also see six stages that likewise build in intensity, rather than diminishing!

As we pass the first half of the month of Av, we encounter an interesting day, the fifteenth of Av, which is described as a yom tov, a holiday. Then we move forward two weeks and we reach the month of Elul. The first day of Elul is not an ordinary day but one of the four days on our calendar that are called a "New Year." It is also a day on which Jewish history and current religious practice overlap. On this day we begin the daily shofar blowing to prepare for the upcoming Days of Awe. It is normative Jewish religious practice to begin preparing for holidays thirty days beforehand. Since the beginning of the month of Elul is thirty days before Rosh Hashanah, then the entire month is concerned with preparing for it, as well as for the other major holidays in Tishrei.

However, as we move backwards in Jewish history, we find a more direct link between this day and the teshuvah process. We know that the Children of Israel gathered at Sinai and received the Torah, in the form of hearing the Ten Commandments, on the sixth of Sivan. Moshe then ascended Sinai to receive the Torah, where he remained for forty days and nights. The day he returned was the seventeenth of Tammuz — which turned very ugly very fast, as he witnessed the people sinning by worshipping the Golden Calf. Moshe reacted by shattering the tablets and then by leading the Tribe of Levi in a cleansing action to deal with the worst of the wrongdoers. Moshe immediately went back up the mountain for an additional forty days and nights to plead on behalf of the Jews. God wanted to destroy the entire nation and essentially start again with Moshe. Moshe passionately argued with God and defended the people. Finally, after those forty days, on the first of Elul, "God relented regarding the evil that He declared that He would do to His people" (Ex. 32:14). Afterwards, Moshe went up for another forty days and nights to receive the Torah again, returning on Yom Kippur. During this time, the Children of Israel were completely preoccupied with repentance and atonement. As we examine this period of teshuvah (repentance), which begins with the first of Elul and reaches its peak on Yom Kippur, we find six distinct stages:

1. The beginning of Elul when we blow the shofar each day and begin our spiritual preparations.

2. At some point during the four to ten days leading to Rosh Hashanah we rise early to recite the *selichot*, penitential prayers, which increase the intensity.

3. Next is Rosh Hashanah itself, the Day of Judgment. On this day (actually two days, or "one very long day," as tradition terms it) we stand before God as our King as He decides our individual fates and the fate of the entire world based on our actions.

4. Next are the days between Rosh Hashanah and Yom Kippur, which, together with the two holidays, form a unit called the Ten Days of Repentance (*Aseret Yemei Teshuvah*). On these days we add special selichot to our prayers, we attempt to live our lives more piously (increasing our participation in prayer, repentance, and charity, in order to lessen or to commute the harsh sentence that would otherwise flow from the judgment of Rosh Hashanah) and we engage in introspection. We also participate in rituals that symbolize our casting off sin or transferring it to another medium.

5. We then encounter the ninth of Tishrei, the eve of Yom Kippur. We use this day to prepare for Yom Kippur by using the mikvah to cleanse ourselves ritually. Additionally, we treat it as a festive day, eating fine food. Our sages teach that "one who

eats and drinks on the ninth is treated as if he fast-
ed both on the ninth and the tenth" (*Berachot* 8a).

6. Finally, we come to Yom Kippur, when that which
was written on Rosh Hashanah is sealed.

Now, what connection is there between this set of six
stages and the six stages of the Three Weeks?

The key is a statement attributed to Rabban Shimon ben
Gamliel: "Whoever eats and drinks on Tishah B'Av is considered as one who would eat and drink on Yom Kippur" (*Taanit*
30b). Lest you think that Rabbi Shimon Ben Gamliel views
Yom Kippur as a day of mourning, that there is a dramatic
connection of sorts between these days, we find this same sage
exclaiming that there is no greater, no more joyous holiday
than Yom Kippur (*Taanit* 4:8). It could well be that the intensity
of this connection is not the similarity of these days, but the
fact that they stand as polar opposites. In fact, Yom Kippur really is the curative for both Shiva Asar B' Tammuz and Tishah
B'Av.

Of the five terrible events of Shiva Asar B' Tammuz, the
one that stands out most of all is the action Moshe took by
breaking the tablets in reaction to the sin of the Golden Calf.
This should have been the day that the Children of Israel received the written Torah. Instead, they received it only eighty
days later, when Moshe descended the mountain with the
Second Tablets. That day was Yom Kippur. In other words, if
Shiva Asar B' Tammuz represents the disease, Yom Kippur represents the cure.

While the first Tishah B'Av was the day that the spies
gave their bad report, the character of the day is defined by its

association with the destruction of both Temples. Both Temples were destroyed on the ninth of Av and the rituals of mourning associated with that day and the entire period of the Three Weeks are related most closely with this aspect of exile. We do not eat or drink on Tishah B'Av, just as we do not eat or drink on Yom Kippur.

However, there once was a Yom Kippur when everyone ate and drank and celebrated — and God blessed the people for their spontaneity. This took place during the celebration surrounding the dedication of the First Temple by King Shlomo. It was the life-long dream of King David, the father of Shlomo, to build a permanent home, a Temple, for God in Yerushalayim. David's life was filled with war and bloodshed, so God would not allow David to construct the Temple himself. Instead He told David that his son would have the merit to oversee the project. Almost immediately after he became king, in the second year of his reign, Shlomo began the project. The construction "officially" began in the fourth year when the foundation was started, and all was completed, without any significant delays, seven years later: "And in the eleventh year, in the month of Bul, which is the eighth month, the house was finished throughout all the parts thereof and according to all the fashion of it, he built it seven years" (I Kings 6:38). The month of completion, the eighth month of the year, called Bul at the time of Shlomo, is the month we now call Cheshvan.

However, the Temple was not inaugurated at that time and services did not yet commence at the site: "And all the men of Israel assembled themselves unto King Shlomo at the feast in the month of *Etanim*, which is the seventh month" (I Kings 8:2). The seventh month is the month of Tishrei. A number of commentators, including the Ralbag and Metsudat David, explain that the term *"Etanim"* is translated as strong and powerful — the month of Tishrei has the strongest and most powerful spiritual effect on the people since it is the month in which Rosh Hashanah and Yom Kippur fall. But when did the festivities commence?

The verses state:

> And Shlomo made a festival at that time and all Israel with him, a great gathering from the entrance of Chamat to the brook of Egypt, before the Lord our God, seven days and seven days, in all fourteen days. On the eighth day he dismissed the people and they blessed the king and went to their homes, rejoicing and delighted of heart for all the goodness that the Lord had done (I Kings 8:65 and 66).

The commentaries interpret this to mean that the festivities commenced seven days before the start of the festival of Succot. This, of course, leads to the obvious question: if they partied for seven days beginning on the eighth of Tishrei, what happened to Yom Kippur, which is on the tenth?

The Talmud in *Moed Katan* (9a) discusses this:

> Rabbi Parnach said in the name of Rabbi Yochanan: That year when Shlomo dedicated the Temple, Israel did not observe Yom Kippur and they were concerned saying, 'Perhaps the enemies of Israel [actually referring to themselves] deserve destruction for this misdeed [eating and drinking on Yom

Kippur].' A Heavenly Voice went forth and said to them: 'You are all prepared for a life in the world to come.'

And from where do we know that He forgave them? Rabbi Tachalifa taught [the verse states]: 'On the eighth day he dismissed the people and they blessed the king and they went to their tents joyful and glad of heart on account of all the goodness that God had done for David, His servant, and for Israel, His people.' When it states "to their tents" it means that they found their wives in a state of purity when they returned home; "joyful," means that they enjoyed the radiance of the Divine presence; "glad of heart," means that each man's wife conceived a male child, and "for all the goodness," teaches that a Heavenly voice went forth and said to them that they are all prepared for life in the world to come.

Thus we see that in the year of the inauguration of the First Temple, the Jews ate and drank on Yom Kippur. This could actually present a new meaning for the statement we quoted from Rabbi Shimon ben Gamliel: "Whoever eats and drinks on Tishah B'Av is considered as one who would eat and drink on Yom Kippur." Rather than focusing on the negative, we can look for the reverse, as well. There is a time when eating on Yom Kippur was appropriate because it was associated with the building of the Temple. Eating on Tishah B'Av will likewise be appropriate when the Temple is rebuilt. Yom Kippur, again, is the antidote to the affliction.

• • • THE NUMBERS EVEN OUT • • •

We thus have a balance in approach (six stages and six stages), we have balance between the fasting and the feasting, and we have balance between destruction and dedication (and ultimately rededication). If you were paying attention, you may have noticed that we had one other balance. Twenty-one/twenty-two/twenty-three days (with the tenth of Av), which seemed to be important in understanding the Three Weeks, were balanced with King Shlomo's festival. The festivities at the dedication are summarized in II Chronicles 7:9 and 10 as follows:

> And they made on the eighth day a solemn gathering, for the inauguration of the altar they made seven days, and the feast seven days. And on the twenty third day of the seventh month, he dismissed the people to their homes...

Thus it seems that King Shlomo ended the official festivities on the twenty-first. The people then spontaneously decided to remain one more day, the twenty–second, as they did not wish to retreat from such joy. Finally, on the twenty-third they returned home, but they also received signs of God's acceptance and favor.

Until we see the Temple rebuilt in its splendor, we will have to understand that while God afflicts us with the pain of the Three Weeks, He balances it with the days of Tishrei. Likewise, while we suffer the affliction of the exile and the consequences of our own sinful actions, we still have our daily prayers, as well as the prayers and holiness of Yom Kippur, to inoculate us against extinction.

• • • ONE IS NOT THE LONELIEST NUMBER • • •

We mentioned how strange it is that we transition back to the regular rhythms of life after the Three Weeks and Tishah B'Av so quickly. The sadness and the rituals associated with mourning built steadily, yet by midday on the tenth of Av, a day on which the Temple was still burning, there is no residual sadness. In fact, historically, the Romans breached the last safe section of the walls of Yerushalayim on the fifteenth and the Jews formally surrendered on the twentieth. Yet we seem to let go immediately. The Shabbat just after Tishah B'Av is in fact rather festive, with a special name, *Shabbat Nachamu*, the Shabbat of Consolation — so named because of the opening words of the *haftarah*, from the book of Jeremiah 40:1, read on Shabbat morning: "*Nachamu nachamu ami yomar Elokeichem* (Comfort, comfort my people — says your God)."

Shabbat Nachamu always coincides with the portion of *Va'etchanan* (Deut. 3:23–7:11). At a glance, this is not a particularly comforting portion. As it opens, Moshe is pleading with God for permission to enter the holy Land of Israel. Moshe carried out every mission, faithfully led the people, and taught them God's Torah. Throughout his entire life he made one little mistake — he hit the rock to provide water for the Jews rather than speaking to it. As a punishment, Yehoshua would lead the people to their home, to the land flowing with milk and honey, in place of Moshe. Moshe, one of the best defense attorneys of all time, who shielded the Jews from God's wrath on many occasions, could not win this one appeal. He would not be allowed to place even one foot in the Land of Israel.

As the portion continues, we reach a section that we read on Tishah B'Av itself, which opens with the lines:

When you beget children and grandchildren and will have been long in the Land, you will grow corrupt and make a carved image of anything and you will do evil in the eyes of the Lord your God and anger Him. I appoint heaven and earth this day to bear witness against you that you will surely perish quickly from the Land to which you are crossing the Jordan to possess; you shall not have lengthy days upon it for you will be destroyed (Deut. 4:24–25).

Not exactly comforting, is it?

The Poetry of Transition

Near the end of summer as vacations wind down and children return from camp, many homes start making the transition to a "back to school" mode. Supply lists pile up, uniform codes, paperwork, and a renewed awareness of summer reading assignments. Yes, what once seemed like all the time in the world — two or more months — has now shrunk to mere weeks. A trip to the bookstore becomes a scavenger hunt for Dostoyevsky, Hugo, Austin, Melville, and a few more recent authors. Noticeably absent from the lists are any poets. There is no Longfellow, Shelley, Keats, Frost, or Whitman.

In today's era of sound and image, a time of instant communication and disposable culture, most people, both consumers and producers, do not seem to have the patience for poetry. The sensitivity, attentiveness, and depth that mark the poet's gift are not valued in the pace of the modern world. Yet, at least religiously, it surrounds us. The *zemirot* (songs) that we sing at our Shabbat tables, the psalms of King David that form the foundation of much of our prayer, and works like the Book of *Eichah* (Lamentations) that we read on Tishah B'Av are written in the language of poetry. "*Eichah yashva badad*" (Alas she sits alone) is line after line of mournful imagery and poetry.

Today, music is really the most popular form of poetic expression. Songs may contain politically charged imagery, like "Blowin' in the Wind," or may contain politically correct feel good messages, as in "We are the World." Songwriters may well be the modern poets. But what, you may ask, does poetry and song have to do with *Shabbat Nachamu* and the portion of *Va'etchanan*? The answer is not "Blowin' in the Wind." Rather it is more of a "Long and Winding Road." The path will connect us with *Va'etchanan*, the Book of *Eichah*, the *Zohar*, and a golden oldie rock and roll classic!

One But Not Only

Perhaps the most apt image from the Tishah B'Av service is that set out in the opening words of Lamentations: "*Eichah yashva badad*" (Alas she sits alone) — the aloneness, the sense of abandonment, the futility. Put another way:

> One is the loneliest number that you'll ever do
> Two can be as bad as one
> It's the loneliest number since the number one
> No is the saddest experience you'll ever know
> Yes it's the saddest experience you'll ever know
> 'Cause one is the loneliest number that you'll ever do
> One is the loneliest number that you'll ever do
>
> It's just no good anymore since you went away
> Now I spend my time

Making rhymes
Of yesterday

One is the loneliest number
One is the loneliest number
One is the loneliest number that you'll ever do
[Three Dog Night from the album Greatest Hits]

In *Va'etchanan*, our great teacher and leader Moshe could have despaired. He could have exited the stage filled with bitterness and disappointment. God seems to be admonishing him like an annoyed parent to a persistent, whining, pestering child: "But God became angry with me because of you and He did not listen to me; God said to me, 'It is too much for you, do not continue to speak with Me further about this matter" (Deut. 3:26). How ironic is it that in this very portion, of the entire Torah, Moshe proclaims and sets out for all of Israel for all time the most important of all proclamations of faith: "Hear O Israel the Lord your God the Lord is One" (Deut. 6:4). Moshe is sending a very important message: God is one, but I, Moshe, am part of that one. I am thus not lonely, I am not abandoned, I am not disappointed — I am complete!

Moshe is linked with Rabbi Akiva, another great teacher of Torah about whom we also read on Tishah B'Av, when in the lamentations in the morning, we recount the story of the execution of ten martyrs. That poem, entitled *Arzei Halevanon* (Cedars of Lebanon) reads:

After him they brought Rabbi Akiva, who uprooted
   mountains
And ground them one against the other by

167

thorough analysis

They combed his flesh with an iron comb in order to break him

His soul departed while he declared '*Echad*' [the last word of the *Shema Yisrael* phrase] and a heavenly voice proclaimed 'Fortunate are you Rabbi Akiva;

Your body has been purified with every type of purity.'

Rabbi Akiva, like Moshe, died at age one hundred twenty. The words of this poem of lamentation relate information set out in the Talmud, *Berachot* 61b, that Rabbi Akiva's soul departed from his body just as he enunciated the word "Echad" upon completing the first verse of the Shema. Nothing could have been more fitting or praiseworthy than returning his soul to that oneness while he was proclaiming it!

While experiencing the pain of the hot rake, understanding that his end was at hand, he did not complain, did not cry or despair. He sought out only one thing; his entire awareness had but one focus — *Echad*, God's Oneness, and the fact that he was a part of it!

But in *Va'etchanan*, Moshe does not move directly from loneliness and disappointment to *Echad*. He detours with a retelling of Matan Torah and a repetition of the Aseret Ha'Dibrot. In other words, he bridges his hurt with Torah. Moshe was Torah. He included this section of Matan Torah because it is a necessary ingredient for the formula of Echad. As the *Zohar* teaches: "*Yisrael, V'oraita, V'Kudsha B'rich Hu Chad Hu*" (Israel, the Torah, and the Holy One Blessed Be He are one). By the time Moshe proclaimed his *Echad*, he had unified all three elements — he was the ultimate Jew, he personified Torah, and he accepted himself and his fate within the oneness of God.

On Tishah B'Av, Israel, — the people and the land, — feels so very alone and desolate. One seems to be the loneliest number. But then Shabbat Nachamu arrives, when we look back to Moshe and realize that we stand as a nation that studies and cherishes Torah and that proclaims, "Hashem Echad," as we lie down and as we rise up. We comprehend this truth, looking at the facts that are otherwise obscured by the pain and the calamities of the exile. We understand that we, Israel, with our holy souls, are a part of Him. This awareness, if achieved, can and should bring us even closer to Him so that He may favor us and the entire world with that day when all will recognize "*Hashem Echad U'Shemo Echad*" (God is one and His name is one).

9

The Connecting Web
Weekly Portions

• • • THE SPACE IN-BETWEEN • • •

We cannot begin to comprehend how God created the world and our universe. Science, despite the rapid advances of the past two centuries, is no closer to the answers. In fact, almost as soon as one theory appears, other evidence or theories emerge that contradict or debunk it. Man, with all of his technology, cannot explore the deepest depths of the oceans on earth and the abundant and varied life that exits there. With our orbiting telescopes and deep space probes, we know so very little about the stars and planets. Even on the simplest and most basic of levels, moving down from molecules to atoms to subatomic particles, our greatest scientists do not understand or agree about how everything holds together.

If you examine any matter closely, you will find that there is a lot more empty space in our reality than there is substance. Modern physicists are researching the "cosmic glue" that holds things together. But if God decided to halt these forces, everything would revert to "null and void." This, in part, may be a useful metaphor for one of the most mysterious aspects of the creation. Our sages teach that the greatest aspect of the miracle of creation was the fact that it was accomplished *"ex nihilo"* (*yesh me'ayin*). One moment there was absolutely nothing besides God. The next there was our tangible reality. God did not create it from existing material. He just created it. But even after He created the tangible, the *yesh*, it would seem that He chose to sustain it only by utilizing the *ayin*, the empty space, the nothingness, the cosmic glue. In a way, despite all we perceive and sense, our reality is all or mainly nothing.

Our lives are a bit like that. We experience a few events or dates that really matter, and a lot of routine nothing. While there are some exceptional individuals who make every day and every minute count, the masses of humanity spend most of their lives just killing time.

Most of our year seems like that as well. There are spiritual times — the holiday seasons — and then there is the undifferentiated mass of existence. If you live with your eyes closed to Torah and the observance of God's commandments, it can be hard to pinpoint the glue of life. It might be relationships, or political causes, or a search for enlightenment, or one of the many other things that give purpose and meaning to people's lives. They seem so real but can be so fleeting.

In my book *Torah 24/7*, I used the Torah as a guide and a year in my life as an example of how God has given us structure and guidance. By studying the Torah as we read it every week, and by living its lessons, we allow God to help us to glue our own lives together. It is the Torah that fills the empty routine spaces, week in and week out, year in and year out. The Torah is the ultimate connection between all of the dates that make up a year. In this chapter, we will examine a few of the types of connections that we find on a macro level within the Torah: how the Torah connects to a cycle of our holidays; how an entire book of the Torah is structured to teach an overriding moral/ethical lesson — just when we need it; and how sections of the Torah connect in both directions, backwards and forwards, to offer up its teachings.

• • • HERE WE GO AGAIN • • •

The Jewish holidays that we celebrate during Tishrei — Rosh Hashanah, Yom Kippur, Succot, and Shemini Atzeret/Simchat Torah — constitute our annual spiritual service call. We get our oil changed, our tires rotated, our transmissions tuned-up, our spark plugs changed, and our batteries recharged. Through the process of teshuvah we seek out faults and festering damage and we repair them, before we experience a serious breakdown. But what fun is having a well-tuned engine without being able to put the top down, the pedal to the metal, and to take a joy ride? We emerge from Yom Kippur and dance right into Succot. We sing, we eat, and we celebrate the Festival of Joy in the great outdoors, no less! Then, it just ends. We go home. We store our succah huts. We properly discard the four species. We reshelve the machzorim. The kids go back to school. We return to work. Everything is just ordinary once again. Or is it?

In Tishrei we experienced four distinct holidays, each with its own character or emphasis. Rosh Hashanah is the New Year, the birthday of the world. It signifies a new beginning.

It was the day on which God created the world. Yom Kippur is the day on which the judgment is sealed. If we repented sincerely, then God grants atonement. If not, then there will be justice, perhaps capital punishment. On Succot we literally depart from the image of stability and permanence that is represented by our homes and show that we have trust in God. During the time of the Temple service, on the seven days of Succot, the Jews brought a total of seventy bulls as a communal offering, signifying their prayers for the welfare of the seventy nations of the world. On Shemini Atzeret, they only brought one bull. This is the day of complete unification with God. After ascending to the spiritual heights represented by the days of the month of Tishrei, God embraces His people — His firstborn son. He holds them one extra day, since parting from them is otherwise so difficult.

But part we do. When the Temple stood in Yerushalayim and the Jews of Israel made their pilgrimages, they packed up and went home (in fact, they likely hurried so as to beat the rains that would start if they prayed successfully). Today, we do the same thing, quickly resuming everyday routines.

The Torah, however, is also a part of this equation. "Israel, the Torah, and the Holy One Blessed Be He are one." The Torah does not want us to roll back downhill to the ordinary so quickly. As we approach the opening weeks of the new cycle of reading, the Torah draws us back into the themes of the holiday season, beginning with the portion from Genesis that contains the story of the first Rosh Hashanah.

We do not commemorate creation on the week we read *Bereishit*. Rather, we study it, discuss it, and analyze it — as we do with every weekly portion. However, because we have experienced Rosh Hashanah itself so recently, the story resonates a little louder. We bring Rosh Hashanah into the cycle of our regular life, not just the special or appointed time.

The next portion, *Noach,* tells the story of a society so corrupt that God judged the world and decided that, except for Noach and his family, it deserved to be destroyed. However, He did not immediately effect His judgment. He told Noach to build an ark. The Tanchuma, cited by Rashi in his commentary, notes that this task took one hundred and twenty years to complete. God hoped that curious people would engage Noach in conversation, learn about the impending flood, and repent. God gave these generations of man not a mere ten days between judgment and sentencing, but one hundred and twenty years. Of course, no one repented. Nevertheless, this story is the template for our Yom Kippur experience. We can choose to repent and be saved or ignore the warnings and wait for God to carry out His original judgment. Yom Kippur is not only the tenth of Tishrei, it is also a part of everyday experience.

If *Bereishit* echoes Rosh Hashanah and *Noach* mirrors Yom Kippur, it follows that *Lech Lecha* will remind us of Succot. By the time we get to this portion, Avraham has settled into a comfort zone. Not only was he no longer persecuted in Charan, he seemed to be thriving. He operated openly to bring people under the wing of God's Divine Presence literally creating souls (Gen. 12:5). He was among family and friends. He may have been out on a limb theologically, but he was otherwise secure. Then one day God tells him: "Go yourself from your land, from your relatives, and from your father's house to the land that I will show you." In other words: leave your safety net and enter the zone of God's protection.

Our actual move may not be as extreme, but we are doing just that — leaving home on God's say so — on Succot. Relying on God's protection and having faith that He provides everything, however, is not limited to Succot. This is a message we relive on the week of the third portion, *Lech Lecha*.

Finally, the unique bond that Avraham forges with God as a result of Akeidat Yitzchak causes God to proclaim: "*Kasha Alai Preidatchem,*" (Your departure from me is difficult). He asks that Avraham just present one more offering, not of you, but for you. He says that their relationship is above what is expected and natural, just like one does not expect a father to offer his son at God's command. The natural world is a world of seven and its multiples: seven days in a week, seventy nations. Eight rises above this, into the realm of the soul and the spirit. Shemini Atzeret is a day when we recapture the emotion and the bonds Avraham experienced. When we read the portion of *Vayeira*, we spill some of this supernatural into our natural.

The four special holidays are followed by four seemingly ordinary Torah portions. They are simply the first four in order. Yet, they can give us the opportunity to reinforce the lessons of Tishrei and to incorporate them into the spaces in-between.

• • • PREPARING FOR BATTLE • • •

The Torah, in a subtle way, thus helps us transition from *kodesh* (holy) to *chol* (mundane) by restating the themes of our holy days — clothing them in different garments, so to speak. We are not forced into abrupt transitions. Rather, the Torah shows us how to imbue the ordinary with the same messages of holiness.

However, everything here is cyclical. The Torah goes

'round and 'round as we read through it each year. Part of what makes the holidays so special is the fact that we have many years of memories and experiences to draw from. Since the Torah helped ease the transition from holy back to mundane at the conclusion of the holiday season, it would not be surprising if we found that it played a role in the otherwise abrupt transition on the other side from mundane back to holy.

In light of the significance of the High Holy Days and the Days of Repentance that lead up to them, there is no shortage of thematic connections between the portions that we read during this time of year (the latter half of the Book of Deuteronomy) and the season. Let's face it, rabbis are devoting much time to these themes and to preparing their communities for the holidays, and when they speak on these weeks, they are likely to look for material from the weekly portions. This is even less of a challenge than one would think because these portions, in fact all of Deuteronomy is something of a spiritual pep talk that Moshe delivers near the end of his life, as he readies the people for their transition into a nation in the Land of Israel. He emphasizes repentance, the importance of choosing good over evil, the supremacy of Torah, and Divine reward and punishment.

Additionally, the imagery invoked in some of the portions lends itself to colorful analogy. One of the best examples of this is an interpretation of the opening line of the portion of *Ki Teitzei*: "When you go out to war against your enemies, and the Lord your God will deliver them into your hand, and you will capture its captivity" (Deut. 21:10). The Baal Shem Tov reads this not as a mere command relating to the rules of warfare. He treats it as a metaphor for the month of Elul, the time of teshuvah. For the Baal Shem Tov the only real enemy can be the *Yetzer Harah*, the evil inclination. He explains: if you rise to battle your evil inclination, know that it is a battle you cannot win by yourself. However, if you make the effort, God will give him up to you. Not only that, this otherwise destructive force will be your captive and will enable you to reach even higher levels of mitzvah observance since your actions will be driven with extra passion and intensity.

As I mentioned, there are many other approaches to integrating the themes of these portions into our preparations for the holidays. However, I recently came across a discourse by a nineteenth century Torah scholar, Rabbi Shlomo Kluger, (1785–1869, Galicia) who uses all of the portions of the entire book of Deuteronomy to deliver a message of ethical preparation. The basic premise that Rabbi Kluger establishes is that our ability to accomplish our goals of teshuvah and *kapara* (atonement) is not through action but through words — prayer! As King David stated in *Tehillim* (Psalms 51:18–19), "You do not want sacrifices, or I would bring them, You do not want burnt offering. The sacrifices of God are a broken spirit; a broken and contrite heart God will not despise." This concept has even more direct expression in *Hoshe'a* (Hosea) 14:3, where the prophet says: "Take with you words and return unto God, say to Him take away all sin and receive us graciously, and we will offer the words of our lips rather than calves."

The two opening portions that bracket Tishah B'Av and are read several weeks before Elul are *Devarim* and *Va'etchanan* — (literally, "words" and "I prayed"). These establish a basic premise: our main supplications will be presented through our words. Knowing this, however, is not the same as understanding how to pray and communicate with God effectively. How can we be sure that He will accept our words? What is the strategy or approach to assure success? According to Rabbi Kluger, the answer is found in the following Mishnah in *Pirkei Avot* (3:1):

> Akavia be Mahalalel said: "Consider three things and you will not come into the grip of sin: know where you came from, where you are going to, and before Whom you will give judgment and accounting." 'Where you came from' — a putrid drop; 'where you are going to' — to a place of dust and maggots; and 'before Whom you will give judgment and accounting' — the King Who reigns over kings, the Holy One Blessed is He.

Thus if a person can retain an awareness of these three concepts while he prays and prepares for prayer on the High Holy Days, then the prayers will have their desired effect.

We find that this message is reinforced as we continue to examine the names of the weekly portions in Deuteronomy:

> *Ekev, Re'eh, Shoftim* (literally, "Intensely, See, Judges") — This is the third factor mentioned in the Mishnah. Think about and see in your mind's eye the judge that you will ultimately be standing before. Feel the intimidation and helplessness of knowing that you will face a court that has a complete record of every sinful action and thought from your entire life and can replay it to your shame and embarrassment.

Ki Teitzei (literally, "when you go out") — This hints at the first factor: where you come from. No matter how rich or smart or powerful you think you are, no matter how much you think of yourself, you are little more than a drop of cloudy liquid. Anything else that you have become, all the characteristics that you have developed, are gifts from God and not reasons to feel haughty or above the restrictions that bind ordinary people.

Ki Tavo (literally, "when you will arrive") — This completes the thought with the second factor: the ultimate destination. We may pursue the pleasures and bounty of this world, but in the end, the bodies that we fed and pampered and worshipped just end up in the dirt, mere feasting for the maggots.

With these thoughts in mind while we pray we can:

Nitzavim (literally, "standing") — Take a stand against the forces that seek to confuse us, distract us, and to prosecute us.

Vayelech (literally, "went") — Then they will depart. You will be left alone with God. Your prayers will be directed to Him without opposition.

Haazinu, V'zot Ha'beracha (literally, "listen" and "this is the blessing") — If you listen to these words of ethical guidance and follow this approach, you will be assured of receiving God's blessing in the upcoming year.

Thus we see that the Torah provides guidance, run-way lights of sorts, to adequately prepare for the Days of Judgment.

• • • BACKWARDS AND FORWARDS • • •

One of the most well known principles applicable to study of the *Chumash* (Five Books of Moses) is *Ein mukdam u'meuchar ba'Torah*, literally, "there is no before or after in the *Torah*" (*Pesachim* 6b). There are times when the Torah seems to be a history book, relating a narrative in chronological order. However, there are many instances where the text deviates from this linear presentation.

For example, in the Book of Exodus, we move forward from a description of slavery in Egypt, through the wonders and drama of the exodus, to the splitting of the sea, and finally to Sinai. However, at this point, the Torah deviates from the story (which would have involved describing the sin of the Golden Calf) and interjects the command to build the Mishkan and its vessels and fixtures. Many commentators note that the command to build the Mishkan, which was given the day after Moshe presented the Children of Israel with the second set of tablets, represented God's grant of atonement and His acceptance of their weakness of spirit. By fashioning the Golden Calf, the people showed that they were not ready for pure spirituality — to actually comprehend having God within them. God thus gave them a tangible symbol — a place where they could comprehend His presence, while He, nonetheless, dwelt within them. In other words, the Torah presents the cure or the repair before the calamitous event. Thus, while the Torah does not constrain itself to chronological order, we find that its order is still very important pedagogically in trying to uncover its teachings.

One place in the Chumash where this is illustrated quite impressively is in the transitions between the weekly portions of *Naso, Beha'alotcha, Shelach,* and *Korach.* At the beginning of each of the latter three portions, Rashi or the Midrash endeavor to explain the connection between sections. Thus, as we move forward we find important moral teachings in the order of the portions itself. What I found to be equally impressive with these portions is that if we attempted to link them not to the next portion, but back to the very beginning of the portion itself, an entirely different, but likewise important, set of lessons emerges. In other words, we can study and connect these sections of the Torah, and the weeks on which we read them, either backwards or forwards!

The latter part of the portion of *Naso,* essentially Chapter 7 of Numbers, details the offerings brought by the tribal princes upon the inauguration of the Mishkan. For twelve days, the princes of every tribe except the tribe of Levi, brought an identical gift. The opening verses of *Beha'alotcha* (Num. 8:1–4) relate the command from God for Aharon to light the Menorah each day in the Mishkan. This seems to be a repeat of a command already related in Exodus 27:21–22. Moreover, it does not seem to relate to the dedication of the Mishkan, the very theme that flows from the end of *Naso.* Rashi, in his commentary on verse 2, asks this very question: "Why does the Torah juxtapose the portion of the Menorah with the portion of the princes?" Rashi answers, citing the *Midrash Tanchuma,* as follows:

For when Aharon saw the role of the princes in the

dedication of the Mishkan he became distressed, for neither he nor his tribe was included with them in the dedication. God said to him, 'On your life [a vow] yours is greater than theirs for you will prepare and kindle the lights.'

The Torah conveys information and fills in the background story through the order of text. In section one, the offerings of the princes, the tribe of Levi and its prince, Aharon, are noticeably absent. Their prominence in the very next section, a section that appears as a non sequitur, teaches us a lesson.

Beha'alotcha concludes with a rather odd event. One day Aharon and Miriam, the second and third greatest prophets and leaders of the Children of Israel in the desert, and Moshe's older brother and sister, had a little family chat. They seemed concerned that Moshe was not paying proper attention to his wife. God reacts immediately by literally "calling them out." He gathers Aharon and Miriam before Moshe to admonish them for speaking ill of Moshe. God then afflicts Miriam with leprosy.

The Torah immediately transitions to the portion of *Shelach*, and the story of the spies that Moshe sent to scout the land. As we know, the spies returned with a negative report, the people despaired, and as punishment, God declared that the generation of the exodus would perish during a forty-year sojourn in the desert.

Rashi, on Numbers 13:2, asks the now-familiar question: "Why is the portion of the spies juxtaposed with the portion of Miriam?" He answers, again citing the *Midrash Tanchuma*:

"Because she was punished on account of the gossip she spoke against her brother and these evil-doers witnessed [her punishment] and were not admonished."

When God afflicted Miriam with leprosy, she was quarantined outside of the camp for seven days. During this time, the people's journey stopped. So great was Miriam, her merit, and the regard and esteem in which she was held by Moshe and the entire nation, that they would not move until she had healed — spiritually. This event was so noteworthy that we are commanded to remember it: "Remember what the Lord, your God, did to Miriam on the day when you were leaving Egypt" (Deut. 24:9). Had the spies heeded this lesson about the impact of their words — especially malicious, destructive words — they could have avoided the punishment. Instead, a whole generation suffered.

At the end of the portion of *Shelach*, the Torah sets out the mitzvah of tzitzit. This mitzvah does not seem to have any connection whatsoever to the text immediately before it, which tells of a man who intentionally violated the Shabbat by chopping wood, and the process by which Moshe determined how he should be punished. More importantly, this section likewise has no apparent connection to the story of the rebellion of Korach that the Torah relates in the portion succeeding it. This next portion is aptly named *Korach*.

After he has explained the grammatical and textual difficulties in the portion and identifies the main characters in this drama, Rashi turns to the narrative problem: why is Korach fomenting a rebellion against Moshe and what method is he employing to attract supporters?

The first part is easy to answer by looking at the family

tree of the tribe of Levi. Levi had three sons: Gershon, Kehat, and Merari. Kehat in turn had four sons: Amram, Yitzhar, Chevron, and Uziel. Amram, being the oldest, received a double portion of honor, in a manner of speaking — one son, Moshe, was the leader or king, and the other, Aharon, was the High Priest. The next honor available was to be the titular head of the families of Kehat. Korach, as the oldest son of the second son, Yitzhar, expected this honor, by right. Instead, Elitzafan the son of Uziel, the youngest of the brothers, received the position. Korach reacted out of vanity and jealousy.

But how, mere months after the exodus and the giving of the Torah, could anyone succeed in challenging the leadership of Moshe? Think of all the miracles, the personal risks, the very fact that he defended them after they sinned with the Golden Calf. He was their leader and their teacher! Korach's gripe was purely personal. So, how did he mount such a serious challenge?

Rashi, citing the *Midrash Tanchuma*, explains and reveals our connection to *Shelach* and the mitzvah of tzitzit at the same time:

> What did he do? He gathered two hundred and fifty Jewish leaders, a majority from the tribe of Reuven his neighbor…and they dressed in four cornered garments (*tallitot*) that were fashioned entirely of turquoise wool [like the one required string in the tzitzit] and they came before Moshe. They said to him, 'Does a tallit that is fashioned completely of turquoise wool require tzitzit or is it exempt?' He said to them, 'It requires tzitzit.' They began to mock

[Moshe], as follows: 'Imagine, a garment made of an entirely different fabric can be exempted with one string, yet this garment which is all turquoise wool cannot exempt itself.'

The very instrument of challenge for Korach was the commandment of tzitzit. Therefore it makes perfect sense for the Torah to present it immediately before describing the conflict between Korach and Moshe.

Thus, as we move forward through these portions, we find that each one connects to the next and we learn details of the narrative that are not apparent from the direct text itself. Even more amazing is that if we take each of these portions and move backwards, connecting the end of the portion to its own beginning, we discover another set of lessons.

The last sections of the portion of *Korach* deal with the tithings that the rest of the Jewish People must give to the tribe of Levi. This section does not seem to have any connection to the narrative portions of *Korach* until the very last verse, which states: "You shall not bear a sin because of it when you raise up its best from it; and the sanctities of the Children of Israel you shall not desecrate, so that you shall not die" (Num. 18:32). The basic command here is that the *kohen* who is receiving the tithe should not offer to help the farmer in return since that demeans the mitzvah. The farmer is required to give because of God's command. There should be no ulterior motives at work. In itself, this could be seen as a commentary or metaphor for Korach, who insincerely used the cloak of religion and piety in order to further his own agenda of jealousy and greed. In *Pirkei Avot* 5:20, Korach's actions are labeled as "a dispute that was not for the sake of Heaven."

But this message, linguistically, is even more direct and stark. Let us repeat those last words again: "...the *sanctities* [kodshei] of the Children of Israel you shall not desecrate, so that *you shall not die.*" Korach hitched his wagon, so to speak, to the notion of the sanctity of the people, "for the entire assembly, all of them *are holy* [kedoshim]" (Num. 16:3). Yet he desecrated that sanctity through his actions. Thus, he died! The end states the lesson of the story at the beginning.

We have already discussed the end of *Shelach*, which explains the mitzvah of tzitzit, and we know that the beginning of the portion recounts the incident of the spies. If we look closely, we again find a linguistic connection between the very end and the very beginning of the portion. This time, Rashi himself even points it out. In Numbers 15:39, the Torah states, by way of explanation for the tzitzit: "...that you may see it and remember the commandments of God and perform them *and not explore* [V'lo taturu] after your heart and your eyes after which you stray." Rashi comments, by way of explaining or translating the unusual term, "and not explore [V'lo taturu] after your heart":

> As in "to explore [mitur] the land" (Num. 13:25);
> the heart and the eyes are the spies for the body,
> procuring sins for it — the eyes see and the heart
> desires and the body commits the sins.

Note the precision of Rashi here. Another variant of the word actually appears in the second verse of the portion, "Send forth men *and let them spy* [V'yaturu] out the land..." (Num. 13:2). However Rashi instead references verse 25, "and they returned *from spying out* [*Mi'tur*] the land ..." In the first reference God gives Moshe permission to send the spies. Obviously, neither God nor Moshe sent them intending a negative outcome. So in this context, their task of spying is benevolent, or at least neutral. Verse 25 describes their return. At this point the die was cast and their intentions were most certainly destructive and harmful. This is the context where we need the protection and reminder of the tzitzit.

The tzitzit are the last word on the incident of the spies. The spies fundamentally erred because they allowed their physical selves — with their very real human emotions, fears, and frailties — to overcome their spiritual beliefs and fortifications. We can all fall prey to such weakness and we all need protection. The section at the end again provides the last word for the narrative at the beginning.

Continuing backward into *Beha'alotcha*, we find the incident where God called Miriam and Aharon to task because they spoke about Moshe. At the beginning of the portion we have the command to Aharon concerning the daily lighting and preparation of the lights of the Menorah. At first glance, there seems to be no connection between the two. However, again we find thematic and textual links.

As we explained above, the transition from *Naso* into *Beha'alotcha* is not obvious or logical. The message we discovered is that Aharon was distressed because he and his tribe were left out of this special part of the festivities. God "comforts" Aharon with the special task of kindling and preparing the lights, and by making a commitment to later generations of his descendants. We can state this another way: Aharon was concerned about his honor and the honor of his family and tribe. It seems as if he felt hurt, slighted, or perhaps self-conscious about his earlier role in the Goden Calf incident. He was concerned about what "people" would think when they noticed that he and his tribe were excluded. He was concerned about public opinion. Is it not interesting to contrast this with his lack of concern for Moshe's honor, with his willingness to listen as Miriam spoke about Moshe in an unflattering way? Where is his sensitivity to honor and family and perceptions and opinion now?

This contrast becomes even more pronounced when we put the events and the text in context: the princes brought their gifts for the Tabernacle from the first through twelfth of the month of Nisan at the beginning of the Jews' second year in the desert, one year after the exodus. During this other-wise festive time, a rather tragic event occurred. On the first of Nisan, Aharon's two eldest sons, Nadav and Avihu, brought a "strange fire" on the altar and God consumed them with fire. At this moment of ultimate joy and at the inauguration of the tangible symbol of God's forgiveness for the sin of the Golden Calf, Aharon, a principle character in that event, loses his sons. This was not intended as a punishment or as retribu-tion against Aharon. In fact, Moshe puts quite a different spin on it: "Moshe said to Aharon, of this did God speak saying, 'I will be sanctified through those who are nearest to Me, thus will I be honored before the entire people,' and Aharon was silent" (Lev. 10:3).

God, for whatever His reason, required these deaths to sanctify the Tabernacle. Thus, Aharon, and by extension his family and tribe, had already given the penultimate gift. The animals and silver of the princes' offerings pale in comparison.

Of special note is Aharon's reaction to the death of his sons. He is silent. He does not speak out against God in any way. He stoically accepts things as they are. In appreciation for this silence, God rewards Aharon in a very sublime way. In Leviticus 10:8–11, we find that God speaks directly to Aharon and transmits a commandment relating to regulation of service by the kohanim. Note the lesson, the cause and effect: Aharon does not speak ill, even when there is real provocation, and God rewards him with direct communication, "*Vaye*daber *Hashem el Aharon le'mor,*" (And God *spoke* to Aharon saying).

As we move ahead to the incident with Aharon and Miriam, let's pay attention to the language. The section begins, "*Va'te*daber *Miriam ve'Aharon b'Moshe…*" (And Miriam and Aharon *spoke* against Moshe…) (Num. 12:1). What is it that emboldens them, and allows them to think that they are sufficiently elevated to judge the actions of a man like Moshe? The answer is in the next verse: "And they said, 'Was it only to Moshe that God *spoke* [*dee'beir*]? Did he not *speak* [*dee'beir*] to us as well?' And God heard." In chastising Miriam and Aharon, he explains the qualitative difference between His conversations with all other prophets (including Miriam and Aharon) and with Moshe. He communicates with all others in dreams, the message given in riddles and metaphors and images. Not so with Moshe. "Mouth to mouth do I *speak* [*adaber*] to him, in a clear *vision* [*mareh*] and not in riddles…." This prompts God to challenge them saying, "Why did you not fear to *speak* [*l'daber*] against my servant Moshe?" (Num. 12:8).

As one reviews these verses, one cannot fail to note how perceptive Rashi is. Perhaps the two most common verses in the Torah, employing the two most common verbs, are 'vayomer X' and 'vayedaber X' ('and X said' or 'and X spoke'). They seem to be used interchangeably and seem to be nothing more than place setters — directing the narrative. There must be several hundred appearances of these verbs. Yet it is in this section, as an introduction of sorts to Numbers 12:1 that Rashi chooses to explain the difference in verb usage.

> The verb "speak" [*dalet-bet-resh*] always appears as a harsh expression, as it says, 'the man [Yosef] who is master of the land spoke to us harshly (Genesis 42:30).' The verb "say" [*aleph-mem-resh*] always is an expression of supplication.

This is where we learn the lessons of speech — nuance, tone, and the meanings and emotions that words convey. There is a reason why the narrative repeats *d-b-r* over and over again. There is a difference in the way God speaks to Moshe and to the others. The failure of Aharon and Miriam to appreciate this led them to misspeak and to be chastised.

As the story plays out, God punishes Miriam with leprosy. Aharon is not punished. Why is he spared the same punishment?

I propose, by flipping back to the beginning of *Beha'alotcha*, that Aharon was indeed punished. Although God did not afflict him physically, he punished Aharon where it would impact him the most, by hurting his feelings. Remember, Aharon received perhaps his greatest reward at a time of intense emotion, because he did not speak. He was silent, so God spoke a mitzvah directly to him.

Despite this reward, and his awareness that he too gave something precious for the dedication, Aharon still felt slighted. He requires assurance from God. Yet this same person did not hesitate to slight Moshe. In fact, the kindness granted by God in speaking directly to him, was actually turned into a negative — a motivating factor in his misjudgment!

Nevertheless, God still acts to assuage Aharon's feelings and to make sure his honor is not tarnished by expressing the commandments relating to the Menorah. But look at the language of this section:

> And God *spoke* [*va'yedaber*] to Moshe *saying* [*le'mor*]. '*Speak* [*daber*] to Aharon and *say* [*ve'amarta*] to him: When you kindle the lamps, toward the face of the Menorah shall seven lights be cast.' Aharon did so; toward the face of the Menorah he kindled its lamps, *as God had commanded to Moshe...* according to the *vision* that God showed Moshe [*ka'mareh asher her'ah*], so did he make the Menorah (Num. 8:1–4).

Even while God is pacifying or calming Aharon, with a reward for generations — a mitzvah that transcends even service in the Temple — the language serves to rebuke him. Aharon, I am not giving you this mitzvah directly, even one so tied to your psyche. I speak to Moshe, who will speak to you! The same one you spoke against! This mitzvah of comfort will forever contain an element of rebuke for Aharon. This is his true punishment, especially as he stands before the vessel, the Menorah, that God showed Moshe in a clear vision, which is so different from the visions that Aharon himself receives. Miriam's punishment lasted a week, although we are commanded to remember it forever. Aharon's was, in a way,

191

forever, even though we do not see it. By linking the beginning and end of *Beha'alotcha,* we learn yet another lesson.

If we looked closely enough we could probably link the entire Torah backwards, forwards, and sideways. However, what we need to do is to link the Torah to our lives every single day. When we are in those in-between times and not so closely connected to the festivals, fasts, and major life events, this is a worthwhile undertaking.

Crown of Jewels
Shabbat and Weekdays

• • • KINGS, QUEENS, AND ANGELS • • •

The more one studies the words and works of the Jewish sages of earlier generations, the more one can appreciate how timeless the tradition truly is. The legal analysis and process of the nearly two-thousand-year-old Talmud is as thorough and sophisticated as modern jurisprudence. The drama and poetry of the books of Tanach have captivated a wider array of readers than any of the classics of literature. The ethical and philosophical works of medieval scholars reflect many ideas that today are labeled cutting-edge. Personally, I am constantly amazed at how modern the outlook of the Midrash is in its creativity, use of language, and its understanding of human behavior.

However, one convention that appears in many of these texts reminds us that these are not the works of twenty-first century minds: the use of parables, metaphors, and analogies of the institution of royalty. In rabbinic literature one will find many stories containing a king and his son or daughter, or loyal retainer, or good friend. Often there will be a betrayal or a meritorious deed, requiring great punishment or reward. Perhaps the king is building a palace, or traveling, or commanding an army, or seeking a spouse for the prince or princess. There are many variations of these themes. We recognize and proclaim God's Majesty many times each day, and so our sages used stories to illustrate the ephemeral relationship between man and God.

Rabbi Shlomo Carlebach (1925–1994), the famous chassidic folk singer and story teller, related a "true" story in the name of the Rebbe from Kubrin that illustrates the themes of the advantages and responsibilities of majesty:

The elder son of one of the czars of Russia, a man himself in line for the throne, once led a coup attempt against his father. The rebellion was quashed and, after a public trial, the son was sentenced to death by the court. The Czar understood that the judgment was correct and had to be carried out. He also loved his son very much and knew that his compassion could be easily aroused. Accordingly, the Czar proclaimed that anyone who would appeal on behalf of the son, or even mention the upcoming execution to the Czar would also be severely punished. Additionally, the Czar appointed a special execution team to transport the son to an undisclosed location outside of the capital on the day of the execution so that there would be no way to stop it.

As luck would have it, the Czar was riding a train on the day of the execution and noticed the execution party out his window. He ordered the train to stop. He got out and approached his son. He said to him, "I regret that you did what you did, and it pains me that you must die. However, I have no choice in this matter. The law is clear and the consequences of your actions are set. There is no room for compassion, despite how much I truly love you."

The son replied, "I understand. I no longer care what you do to me. However, I have but one request. We still have a few miles to go before we reach the site of the execution. I would like you to ride with us so that I can walk ahead of you and shout, 'Our master the Czar should live forever!'"

The Czar granted this request. Of course, after riding several miles and listening to his son proclaim his majesty and legacy, when they reached the destination, the Czar could no longer allow the execution. Being a prince exacerbated his predicament and required the strictest of punishments, but it also provided the key to his salvation.

But princes are not the only ones who have this special quality. God, indeed, chooses to honor us with majesty on a daily basis. This is not a mere metaphysical concept — we literally place His crown on our heads every day.

What is this crown? When did we receive it? How has it evolved? What does it represent?

• • • THE CROWNS OF MAJESTY • • •

If majesty comes directly from God and is, in fact, a portion of God's own sovereignty, then the place to start is with God, Himself. We know of God's chariot and throne from the prophecies of Yechezkel, but what do we know of God's crown?

One possible understanding comes from a rather unique interaction between God and Moshe immediately after the sin of the Golden Calf. Between the sixth of Sivan and Yom Kippur of that first year in the desert, Moshe spent a lot of time in the heavens with God — forty days for the first Tablets, forty days to defend the Jews, and forty days for the second Tablets. Near the end of the second forty-day period, when God capitulates and agrees not to destroy all of the Jews and start a new nation from Moshe, Moshe has reached a pinnacle of spirituality. He speaks to God face to face, and is at that moment closer to God than any creation has ever been.

At this moment, Moshe makes an amazing request. He wants to see God's "Glory." God responds that no man can see God's Face and live (Ex. 33:20). Instead, He offers Moshe a slightly lesser alternative. Moshe will sit on a rock and be shielded by God's hand as God passes before him. At the moment of God's passing, He will remove His hand and allow Moshe to see His back.

But if God has no corporeal presence, what is Moshe seeing? Why does Moshe even ask to see something that doesn't exist? What is the difference between the front of God, His hand, and His back? And what does he actually see?

The Talmud, *Berachot* 7a, explains as follows: "Rabbi Channa bar Bizna said, 'To what does the verse refer when it states "and you will see my back?" This teaches that God showed Moshe the knot of tefillin.'" In other words, God "wears" tefillin on His head. This is God's crown.

One folio earlier, Berachot 6a, the Talmud discusses God's tefillin. A number of sages, bringing proofs from Biblical verses, establish that God does "wear" tefillin. However, this leads to a significant question: the tefillin that we wear every day contain four selections from the Torah: *Shema* (Deut. 6:5-9), *Vehaya im shamo'a* (Deut. 11:13–21), *Kadesh li kol bechor* (Ex.

13:1–10), and *Vehaya ki yevi'acha* (Ex. 13:11–16). Each of these sections deals with the obligations of the Jews to perform mitzvot. God does not have these obligations and needs no such reminders. Therefore, Rabbi Nachman bar Yitzchak explains that God's tefillin contain a different set of passages that correspond to the ones in our tefillin. These passages deal with God's esteem for His people — our uniqueness, our praiseworthiness, and God's commitment to us.

When did we receive our crowns? When were we elevated to royalty? These questions are answered by the Talmud in *Shabbat* 88a:

> Rabbi Simai explained: At the moment the Jews said, 'We will do' (*naaseh*) before, 'We will hear' (*v'nishma*) 600,000 ministering angels descended, one for each Jew, and they tied two crowns on each head, one for 'we will do' (*naaseh*) and one for 'we will hear' (*v'nishma*). However, when the Jews sinned, 120,000 destructive angels descended and they removed the crowns...and in the future God will return them to us, as it says (*Yeshayah* 35:10), 'And the ransomed of the Lord shall return and come to Zion with songs and everlasting joy [*simchat olam*] and gladness; and sorrow and sighing shall flee'— a joy that for all times will be on their heads [*simchah shemeolam al rosham*].

At Sinai the Children of Israel became the priestly nation; they were crowned and adorned by the angels themselves. However, it seems that by sinning, they lost their crowns. Yet we, as established above, wear crowns each day — the same crown that God wears. How do we reconcile this with the notion that the angels removed our crowns?

The key to understanding our crowns may be found in a Midrash (*Devarim Rabbah* 3:7) that, not surprisingly, discusses kings, queens, and crowns. This Midrash tells the story of a queen who brought with her two precious jewels as a dowry when she married the king. The king matched her dowry with two more jewels. But when the queen lost her two jewels, the king took his back and only when she found hers again did he return his, proclaiming that all four jewels would now be used to make a crown for the queen to wear.

This is analogous to Avraham's relationship to the Jewish People. His gifts to his children and grandchildren were charity (*tzedaka*) and justice (*mishpat*). God, like the king, matched those two gifts with kindness (*chessed*) and mercy (*rachamim*). But when the Jews sinned at the Golden Calf, they lost their sense of judgment, and God in turn took away his kindness and mercy to punish them. Only when they repented did they regain their original jewels along with God's. Once this was achieved, God, like the king, decided to fashion these four jewels (in the form of the four passages we mentioned above) into the "crown" of tefillin, which the Jews would wear as a holy reminder of their past.

Finally, if we compare the last verses of the Talmud passage and the Midrash that explains it, we find another fascinating connection. The Talmud concluded by interpreting the words from *Yeshayah* to mean, "a joy that for all times will be on their heads," [*simchah sheme'olam al rosham*]. Olam (for all times) means forever. When God makes a statement, it must be true. Thus, if He says "forever"...it must mean forever. There is no past, present, or future for God — there is just forever. In other words, while we may think that the crowns are gone and that we have lost a share of Divine Majesty, this is just misdirection. We wear the crown, with all four jewels nearly every day.

We learn this from the verse that the Midrash concludes with, the verse from *Hoshe'a*: "I will betroth you to Me forever, and I will betroth you to Me with *righteousness, justice, kindness, and mercy*. I betroth you to Me with fidelity and you shall know God" (*Hoshe'a* 2:21–22). This is not an obscure passage. This is a passage that we recite every time we put on our tefillin. The passage refers to the betrothal between God, our King, and the Jewish People. We reinforce this relationship as we wrap the straps around our finger, like the placement by a groom of a wedding ring on his bride's hand.

Yet, as we learned in the Midrash, the significance of this passage is its reference to the four jewels — God's two and our two — that adorn the crown that the king gives the queen. The tefillin that we place on our head contain four Torah sections. However, unlike the design of the tefillin on our arm where all four sections are written on one scroll and placed in one chamber, the *tefillin shel rosh* have four chambers into which we place four separate scrolls of parchment. In other words, the design corresponds to the crown described in the Midrash, with the four jewels of righteousness, justice, kindness, and mercy — and we know that this is a crown, because this is what God showed Moshe as representing the adornment on God's head.

• • • WHAT'S IN A SIGN • • •

Considering how special and important tefillin are and how much they are identified with prayer, it is puzzling why we do not don them on the Shabbat, the holiest day of the week. Yet the law is clear: we do not use tefillin on the Shabbat, and in fact, they are even *muktza*.

Rabbi Akiva explains (*Menachot* 36b) that when we read, "and they shall be for you as a sign (*ot*) on your hand" (Ex. 13:9), this means that one only needs a sign when he otherwise lacks one. Because the Shabbat and festivals are, in and of themselves, signs, we do not need additional ones. Some add that the concept of a sign is related to testimony — affirmation by the Jew of the ot is an acceptance of Torah and mitzvot. Jewish men always have one ot present, the ot of the circumcision (*brit milah*), thus only one additional ot is needed. On weekdays this is the ot of tefillin. On Shabbat and festivals it is the ot of the days themselves. So the key to understanding an important connection between ourselves, the ordinary weekdays, and the Shabbat is contained within this concept of ot. More specifically, we find the answers contained within the letters of the word itself.

The first verse of the Torah sets forth the act and method of creation. "*Bereishit* (in the beginning), *bara Elokim* (God created) et [*aleph-tav*] *hashamayim v'et* [*aleph-tav*] *ha'aretz* (the heaven and the earth)" (Gen. 1:1). The word "et" in this verse has no translation. It represents God's primary tool — the twenty-two letters of the Aleph Bet, from *aleph* through *tav*.

When God created the world with the twenty-two letters of the Aleph Bet, he did so with *din*, justice. The very word referencing God in the first verse is *Elokim*, which means Judge.

His creation started with the *tav* and finished with the *aleph*. We see this hinted at in the endings of the opening words: *BereishiT barA* — tav, then aleph. We also see this from the timing of creation. Recorded time began on the first day of Tishrei. The name for this month, which is also the month during which God annually judges the world, is spelled tav-shin-resh-yud — the first three letters of the reverse Aleph Bet, the Aleph Bet of din, with the possessive *yud* added.

However, man cannot exist in the world of strict din. From almost the first moments of creation man proved that he would exercise free will in a manner inconsistent with God's commands and thus would earn constant punishment and destruction. Man can only survive in a world of mercy, *rachamim,* which moves forward from *aleph* to *tav*. The letters themselves reflect this character as evidenced by the fact that we immediately encounter the word "*av*" (*aleph-bet*), the Hebrew word for father, indicative of the fact that the mercy of God is like the mercy of a father for a child.

The word ot, the center of our discussion, is comprised of three Hebrew letters, *aleph-vav-tav*. Every ot that God gives to man contains the *aleph* to *tav* indicative of *rachamin* ... with one extra letter, the *vav*.

Vav is a very important letter in its own right, especially in this context. *Vav* is man as can be explained in two simple ways. First, God created man on the sixth day of creation (the gematria, numerical equivalent, of *vav* is six). Second, we proclaim daily in the *Shema* that God is One. What does *vav* mean in Hebrew? It generally connotes the word "*and.*" When God created man, suddenly there was a new relationship in the universe, that of God and that which He made God-like by placing a part of Himself, a holy soul, into a vessel. Thus there is now God *and* man! Every ot connects God as manifest in the attribute of rachamim to man. Thus, each ot is important.

In the portion *Noach*, in connection with the story of the rainbow (*keshet*) we find the term ot accompanying a *brit* (covenant). The concept of brit is far more ephemeral and esoteric than that of ot. A brit is something that is a complete intangible — a deal, a covenant, a promise between parties.

In civil law, one loosely perceives a contract as involving a meeting of the minds. But do two human minds ever fully meet, or do they differ in preconception, self-interest, and ego? Now consider the gulf between a human mind and the Divine. Brit may well be needed to provide the framework in order for there to be an agreement with God, in contrast to a command (*tzivui*) from God. However, ot, especially within the realm of man/God interaction, is needed to provide an objectification of the deal.

But even there we get ahead of ourselves. Is it not presumptuous to think that God makes and is bound by convenants with man? Can there be equal bargaining position? God knows what is in the hearts and minds of mankind and what all future conduct and performance will be. Moreover, God is truth (*emet*) and would never be accused of inconsistency or non-performance or be held accountable for breach.

These arrangements or convenants are thus simply gifts to us — to the individual man, to mankind, or to the Jewish People, depending on the particular ot. They are links to God, connections. They are not required in a strict sense. Our Lord/King/Master could rightfully demand/command agreement/performance. Accordingly, any such relationship is, by definition, contracted with mercy (rachamim) rather than strict justice (din).

After Noach and his family emerged from the ark, he offered a series of sacrifices to God. In response, God blessed Noach and made a number of promises and commitments to him, including one that He would never again destroy the world by flood. In connection with this promise, God provided an eternal sign of this commitment:

> And God said, 'This is the sign of the covenant (ot brit) that I give between Me and you and every living thing that is with you for generations forever. I have set My rainbow in the cloud and it shall be a sign of the covenant (ot brit) between Me and the earth' (Gen. 9:12–13).

The rainbow, this first ot brit, is introduced in Genesis 9:13 with the words "*Et kashti*" [*aleph-tav, kuf-shin-tav-yud*] — "My Rainbow." The word *et* here, as in the first verse of *Bereishit*, has no translation or grammatical function — to signify that God is once again employing the *Aleph Bet* of rachamim. This is especially important since the very word/symbol chosen for this particular brit is the consecutive letters *kuf-shin-tav* (the *yud*, again, is a possessive pronoun), a representation of rachamim in the letter form. God would want to impart this message that there will be mercy on a devastated world to the very end. But note that this particular sign was not intended solely for Man.

In terms of our objective experience, a rainbow is formed by the interaction of water and light. When was light created? You might jump the gun and respond, "On day one," ("Let there be light"). But according to many midrashic sources, God hid that light. The light that we experience, the light that illuminates our existence, is the light of the luminaries that were created on Day Four. The same luminaries that God described would be used "*l'otot*" (as signs), written *aleph-tav-tav,* without the *vav* of man (Gen. 1:14). The brit of the keshet, the rainbow, thus contains no direct aspect of Divine holiness or spirituality. It is the product of two natural creations, water and light. This is as it should be, since this brit is with "*kol chai*" (all living things) and not solely with man, the *vav.* Creation does not respond to the supernatural in any meaningful way. Nature is literally grounded in the earth, not the spirit.

Man is unique among all creation (above and below) in that he represents the only fusion of physical and holy — *guf* and *neshamah* (body and soul). Any brit for man alone by definition requires both elements.

The best example of this is three important convenants/signs that God established with the Jewish People: circumcision (*milah*), phylacteries *(tefillin),* and the Sabbath (*Shabbat).* These three otot differ from the ot of the keshet because two dimensions (physical and spiritual) are integrated within them, rather than one. Thus God accomplishes something quite unique with these three signs.

There is an interesting progression at work in these early portions of Genesis. In *Bereishit* we encounter the ot (Gen. 1:14). In the portion of *Noach* the ot brit with kol chai (Gen. 9:12). In the third portion, *Lech Lecha,* we have ot brit only with man, which I will call a brit with an ot. If we compare Gen. 17:1–14 with Gen. 15:7–21, we may discover God's intention for the ot with man.

The first section is known as the *Brit Bein Habetarim* (The Covenant between the Parts [P]). The second is the *Brit Milah* (Covenant of Circumcision [C]). If you read both superficially they seem merely to repeat. Yet, upon closer examination, the differences are quite significant.

1. In P, God appears in the text completely as rachamim (*Y-H-V-H*) after his initial introduction as "*Kel Shakkai*." In C, He appears as din (*Elokim*), after a repeat of *Kel Shakkai* and an initial address as rachamim.

2. P involves or requires no direct commitment from Avraham. In C, on the other hand, he literally must surrender a piece of his body.

3. In P, God does not give Avraham anything. In C, God gives Avraham a priceless gift: direct association between God and Avraham, symbolized by the fact that God added a letter of his name, the *heh*, to Avram's name. He is now AvraHam.

4. In P, rachamim is harsh and logical, tit-for-tat — four hundred years of slavery for Avraham's children in exchange for the bounty: great treasure. In C, din is expansively gracious, promising the Land of Israel, leadership over the nations, and prosperity.

5. In P there is *anan* (clouds — water!) and *aish* (fire). In C, neither appears.

6. In P there is no ot. In C there is the ot of milah.

Cutting to the chase, P represents a brit between God and man, but C represents a brit between God and the Jewish People. The other nations of mankind, as witnessed in the creation and the flood, cannot covenant with din. They are one dimensional, relating to God physically rather than spiritually. Even their spiritual encounters are defined physically. For example, even after entering into to the covenant with God, after witnessing the flood and receiving the ot brit of the keshet, Noach is described as follows: "Noach, *the man of the earth,* debased himself and planted a vineyard" (Gen. 9:18). When God describes the ot brit after the flood, he merely lumps Noach with kol chai, all living things. In contrast with Avraham, the first Jew, Noach was not spiritually ready to enter into a covenant relationship with God by himself as a man.

Without a relationship with din, these nations can never be linked to Torah. At Sinai, God establishes the terms, the holy equation: *"Anochi Hashem Elokecha"* — One = rachamim and din. This is the same formula each Jew must recite as he lies down to sleep and arises for the day: *Hashem Elokeinu* (rachamin and din) = Echad (One).

A brit is just a deal: do this, get that. However, a brit represented or connected with a personal ot, links man with the Divine. After all, man is *Tzelem Elokim* (God's Image). The "Big Three" covenants show us how this works.

God is non-corporeal (*"Ein lo demut haguf, v'eino guf"* — He has no semblance of body and is not corporeal). Yet, He chooses for us to bind with Him using our own bodies in milah. The message is direct. Our bodies, which we believe to be "dust and ashes," essentially just mere shells for our immortal souls, are (or can be) transformed into pure spirituality. If this were not so, why would *techiyat hameitim* (resurrection of our bodies at the end of days) a basic tenet of religious faith, be necessary?

Next, God is outside of time (*haya, hoveh, v'yihiyeh* — was, is, and will be). With the ot of Shabbat, which represents sanctified time, we again learn and experience that a realm we thought was purely physical can be sanctified and elevated to the spiritual.

Finally, we have tefillin. What are the human analogues to din and rachamim? Logic and emotion, or the head and the heart. The tefillin link these human symbols to the Divine.

The message should, by now, be clear. God, the Torah, and the Jewish People are bound together with multiple levels of symbol, structure, and connection (ot brit). As you take the mental equivalent of a microscope to any component and look at the words (molecules) and letters (atoms) utilized by our Creator to fashion this world and our religion, truth and clarity emerge.

The Path of the Just

A Complete Year

• • • READING BETWEEN THE LINES • • •

Many of the relationships and connections that form the thematic core of this book started out as questions, observations, or inspirational realizations that I came upon while studying Torah. In *Pirkei Avot* (5:26), the sage Ben Bag Bag counsels: "Delve in the Torah and continue to delve in it, for everything is in it." The principle way of digging is by asking questions. Questioning even the most basic and accepted premises often leads to new paths of discovery. Many of the chapters of this book were inspired by such basic questions. The answers led down winding pathways that often explained deeper levels of a holiday or period of time. Other themes appeared from observing — just paying attention to language or imagery, or numerical relationships, or characteristics of personality. Likewise in these instances, initial recognition led to the discovery of a pattern or structure. I have been able to fill chapters with my attempts to provide answers to the questions and to describe the patterns disclosed by observation.

Throughout this book, we have discovered the connections between different holidays and holiday seasons and between the Torah portions and the times of the year in which we read them. We've been moving from the macro — holiday seasons and overarching themes to the micro — how the flow of our week is intimately connected to the larger patterns of the year. What I would like to do now is to explore the breakdown of our daily lives and see how we can ultimately put it all together.

• • • EIGHTEEN DIVIDED BY • • • THREE EQUALS SEVEN

When a source of Jewish law uses the term *tefillah* (prayer), one must pay extra attention to the context. Sometimes the word is used to describe the activity and sometimes it is used to describe one particular component of daily prayer, the *Amidah* or *Shemoneh Esrei* (Eighteen Benedictions). The *Amidah* is central to every one of the three daily prayer services, and is recited four times on Rosh Chodesh, Shabbat, and Holidays to account for the extra *Musaf* offerings brought in the Temple on those days. It is also recited five times on Yom Kippur, when we add a concluding service called *Ne'ila*.

You may have noticed that there are two common terms for this prayer: *Amidah* and *Shemoneh Esrei*. This is because, while it is always said b'*amidah* (while standing in place, feet together, for the duration of the prayer), it does not always consist of eighteen blessings. Its present form consists of nineteen blessings — the original eighteen plus a nineteenth, *V'lamalshinim* (the Slanderers), added nearly five hundred years later, after the destruction of the Second Temple, by the yeshiva of Rabban Gamliel II in Yavne (*Berachot* 28b).

We recite the full *Shemoneh Esrei* during each of the three regular weekday services. However, on the Shabbat, as well as on most festivals, the prayer consists of seven blessings.

It is interesting to note that the Talmud discloses similar sources for the number of blessings associated with the week-day and the Shabbat *Amidah* prayers, respectively. In *Berachot* 28b, Reb Hillel ben Reb Shmuel ben Nachmani answers that the eighteen weekday blessings correspond to the eighteen times that God's Name appears in Psalm 29. In *Berachot* 29a, the Talmud discloses that the seven blessings on the Shabbat correspond to the seven times that Psalm 29 references the "Voice" of God.

The number seven appears in many places and typically represents a complete cycle or a total system. Seven is also the number of the Shabbat itself — it is *Yom Shevi'i* (the seventh day). God created the world in six days and rested on the seventh. Thus, there is logic to having seven blessings associated with the prayers of Shabbat. But, what about the eighteen? Eighteen is a significant number in Judaism. It represents life: *chai* (*chet* [8] and *yud* [10]). This may seem simplistic, but I believe the significance of the number eighteen, quite simply, lies in the weekdays, just as the seven "rested" in the Shabbat itself. There are six weekdays. We pray three times a day, for a total of eighteen prayer services. Thus eighteen encompasses or captures the notion of prayer for the week.

This notion fits well with the discussion of the origin of the three prayer services, *Shacharit* (morning service), *Mincha* (afternoon service), and *Arvit* (evening service). In the Talmud

(*Berachot* 26b), Reb Yose b. Reb Chaninah states that the *Avot* (forefathers) established these prayers: Avraham established Shacharit, Yitzchak established Mincha, and Yaacov established Arvit. In the *Talmud Yerushalmi* (*Berachot* 4:3), Rebbi Chaninah said in the name of Rebbi Pinchas that the eighteen blessings correspond to the eighteen times the names Avraham, Yitzchak, and Yaacov appear as a unit in the Torah. Putting these two thoughts together, if each of the three Avot prayed three services each of the six weekdays, this would be eighteen.

• • • ETHICAL UNITY • • •

When we think of tefillah, we think of consistency, devotion, and the formalizing of a way of life. As we just saw, the prayer services are not randomly composed, and they affect us on a deep level even in their very structure. At this point, it should be clear to you that nothing in Judaism is random or insignificant. It is important now to look at the bottom line: what is the message, the ultimate lesson, that we are trying to learn through our lives as Jews?

Many rabbis have hypothesized on the meaning of life, but none has done so more successfully than Rabbi Moshe Chaim Luzzatto (known as "Ramchal," 1707–1747, Italy and Israel) in his book entitled *Mesilat Yesharim*, "The Path of the Just." This book is considered to be the foremost text on Jewish *mussar* (ethics and character development). What makes this book so popular is the fact that its depth and profundity is cloaked in a very straightforward approach. Moreover, the language is a classical Hebrew that is almost simple in its clarity.

The book is a step-by-step guide to improving one's character and to achieving lofty spiritual goals. Ramchal organized the book in concert with a teaching of R' Pinchas ben Yair, a sage of the era of the *Mishnah*, who is quoted in *Avoda Zara* 20b. This teaching is as follows:

> Torah leads to watchfulness (*zehirut*); watchfulness leads to diligence (*zerizut*); diligence leads to cleanliness (*nekiut*); cleanliness leads to abstinence (*prishut*); abstinence leads to purity (*taharah*); purity leads to piety (*chassidut*); piety leads to humility (*anavah*); humility leads to fear of wrongdoing (*yirat chet*); fear of wrongdoing leads to sanctity (*kedushah*); sanctity leads to holy spirituality (*ruach hakodesh*); and holy spirituality leads to resurrection (*techiyat hameitim*).

Ramchal's method is to explain each characteristic, to define the components of each characteristic, to describe how one acquires each characteristic, and to warn against that which diminishes the characteristic. The book can be studied within a short span of days or weeks. Yet it likely would take a lifetime to master and apply.

But despite its surface simplicity, I began to see a larger connection to the order of *Mesilat Yesharim* as I researched this book. What I discovered was that all of these characteristics are related to God's plan for our spiritual growth and development, otherwise known as the *mo'adei hashanah* (the festivals of the year) as related in the Torah. As we review the structure of the holidays written in Leviticus 23:1–44, as set out with a precise order and an emphasis on particular characteristics, we will discover some enlightening parallels to the Ramchal's philosophy. Remember, Ramchal's starting point is Torah; Torah leads to the path of the various characteristics. What could be better than finding a guide to these characteristics in one section of the Torah! As Rashi says, we are required to make festivals "so that Israel may be educated through them." Thus, the holidays themselves are designed and structured to teach us the most important spiritual lessons of all.

Shabbat and Zehirut

God, through Moshe, begins to teach about the holidays in a rather unusual way. In Leviticus 23:2, the topic is described as, "God's appointed festivals that you are to designate as holy convocations." This is generally understood to mean that while the holidays are Divinely commanded, God has delegated to man (within limits) the ability to establish the actual times for the holidays as a part of the regulation of the calendar. Nevertheless, the very first holiday listed is the Shabbat, which is fixed and established (every seventh day) and not dependent on the calendar. Thus we see from the start that this portion is doing something more than just informing us about the holidays. It is creating a list of specific times and days, with their own characteristics.

There are two basic aspects to the Shabbat, as represented by the two versions of the command relating to the Shabbat on the two sets of Tablets. One command is *zachor* (to commemorate/remember) and the other is *shamor* (to observe/safeguard). In the *Lecha Dodi* prayer each Friday night we proclaim: "*Shamor v'zachor b'dibur echad,*" (Safeguard and remember in a single utterance). This means that while it seems that there were two separate commands regarding the Shabbat, God actually presented them simultaneously. Zachor represents the affirmative or positive aspect of proclaiming the holiness of the Shabbat — singing, praying, reciting the kiddush, treating it as a special day. Shamor, on the other hand, is the obligation to avoid desecrating the Shabbat by performing certain acts of work or of creative effort — it is the negative aspect of the mitzvah.

The verse in Leviticus (23:3) stresses only one aspect of the Shabbat: "The seventh day is a day of complete rest; *you shall not do any work....*" In other words, we must guard against and avoid any act that could lead to any possible transgression of the Shabbat. The essence of safeguarding Shabbat is zehirut, watchfulness; the first of the characteristics on Ramchal's list. Moreover, within any scheme of improvement, reaching the first level is always the hardest. Thus by linking the first characteristic with the weekly Shabbat we are given the greatest of all opportunities to learn the lesson and to start on the path towards spiritual growth.

Pesach-Zerizut and Nekiut

In verse 4, the Torah signals another transition. We are presented with yet another introduction, a proclamation regarding the appointed festivals of God that basically repeat verse 2. Now, we are moving into a description of the days that we term holidays, starting with Pesach. If you look closely at verses 5–8 you will notice that there is actually a lot going on. On the afternoon of the fourteenth day of the first month we have a day called "Pesach to God." On the fifteenth day we have a holiday called the Festival of Matzot. On this day work is prohibited.

We are then told that we should eat *matzah* for seven days and bring special offerings. Finally, on the seventh of these days, we have another day on which work is prohibited.

As we unravel these verses, it seems as if there are two focal points — the transition between the fourteenth and the fifteenth (with the holiday on the fifteenth) and the twenty-first (the seventh day, the other holiday). The afternoon of the fourteenth is the time for bringing the Paschal sacrifice. The meat will actually be consumed on the eve of the fifteenth. Nevertheless, as the holiday really begins, the focus is not on the Pesach, but on the matzah. It takes much effort to remove the chametz and to create an environment that is *"kulo mat-zah"* (only matzah). But it is more than just the physical effort of scrubbing, cleaning, and searching. It involves the ultimate in zeal, in zerizut. From the moment you mix the water with the flour you have eighteen minutes to complete the baking process. Even one second more can result in chametz. Matzah is thus the embodiment of zerizut. The beginning of the festival teaches us to refine the characteristic of zeal.

In addition to this, there is another interesting aspect to the mitzvah of matzah. Our sages teach that we are only obligated to eat matzah, from the standpoint of fulfilling a positive command, on the first day of the holiday. For the rest of Pesach, while we certainly may eat matzah, we are subject only to a command *not* to eat chametz. Thus as we face the end of the festival, represented by the seventh day, our pride is in the fact that we stayed clean, we avoided the taint, we did not allow chametz into our possession during the festival. Cleanliness is the very next characteristic.

Omer and Prishut

We have noted that this section contains not one, but two verses introducing this portion as dealing with the holidays: verses
2 and 4. Yet as we move past Pesach, we do not encounter the
next holiday, Shavuot, but instead we take a detour into the
laws of the Omer period. The next characteristic from *Mesilat
Yesharim* is prishut, abstinence or separation. If we think historically about this seven-week period between Pesach and
Shavuot we will see that this was precisely what the days represented. The Jews left Egypt steeped in the idolatrous culture
of their environment. They were not Jews; they were freed
Egyptian slaves. Left to their own devices, they likely would
have established their own independent existence on a model
of Egyptian life. Before they would be ready to receive God's
Torah and be ready to embark on new and different lives they
required intense and total seclusion and isolation. They needed to withdraw and abstain from everything that they knew. It
is interesting that according to Torah law, when a woman becomes impure because of a menstrual discharge she must actually count seven clean days before she may reunite with her
husband. Similarly, before our own wedding night on Sinai,
we also counted a period of separation — in this case seven
weeks — before we could unite with God.

Shavuot and Taharah

When the Jews left Egypt they were on the forty-ninth level
of impurity. They could not receive the Torah in such a state.
After the Omer days in the desert, they finally reached the requisite state of purity. They thus arrived at the first Shavuot, the
next holiday on the list, in a state of taharah, the next charac-

teristic on the list. As we have noted previously, the culmination of the redemption from Egypt was not the day they left, Pesach. Rather, God specifically told Moshe at the very outset, "...and this is your sign that I have sent you; when you take the people out of Egypt you shall serve (*ta'avdun*) God on this mountain" (Ex. 3:12). Accepting and receiving the Torah was the ultimate service of God by the Jewish People. It is interesting that in the blessing that we recite during the Shabbat and festival Amidah we ask God to "sanctify us with Your commandments and grant us a share in Your Torah...and purify (*v'taher*) our hearts to serve You (*l'ovdecha*) sincerely." Service of God, with Torah and mitzvot is a function of taharah, and is the essential lesson of Shavuot.

Rosh Hashanah and Chassidut

Next, the Torah describes the holiday we call Rosh Hashanah. The only image that is conveyed in connection with the holiday is the sounding of the shofar. The shofar is the lingering remembrance of the Akeidah (Binding of Yitzchak), the ultimate test passed by Avraham to establish his entitlement to our spiritual heritage. Avraham is associated with the characteristic of *chessed* and chassidut more than any other person. Therefore, Rosh Hashanah must be the holiday of chassidut.

However, there is a more direct connection between chassidut and Rosh Hashanah found in the liturgy for the holiday. The third blessing, which proclaims the holiness of God's name, is the shortest of all the blessings we recite in the regular Amidah. However, on the *Yamim Nora'im* ("Days of Awe") it is expanded to include aspects of God's majesty. One of the paragraphs in this expanded blessing reads as follows:

And so too the righteous (*tzadikim*) will see and be glad, the upright (*yesharim*) will exult, and the pious (*chasidim*) will be mirthful with glad song. Iniquity will close its mouth and all wickedness will evaporate like smoke, when you remove evil's dominion from the earth.

The *Artscroll Rosh Hashanah Machzor* (p. 66) offers the following comment:

These three categories are in ascending order. Righteous people are those who obey the commands of the Torah even though they may be strongly tempted not to, or they may not understand the justice of God's ways. Upright people are those whose faith is so perfect that they never question God's will or ways....(*Sfas Emes*). The devout (pious) are those who seek to serve God *by doing more than the minimum requirements of the law;* in effect they do chessed (kindness) with God, so to speak (*Zohar*) [Emphasis mine].

Chasidim are the ones who reach the highest level of proclaiming the majesty of God on Rosh Hashanah. What is most fitting about this is that they are defined by a particular characteristic, living their lives in a manner that is *more than the minimum requirements of the law (lifnim mishurat hadin)*. Rosh Hashanah is the Yom Hadin, the ultimate Day of Judgment. Thus, this is the day that is most fitting to develop the characteristic that calls for justice and more, the trait of chassidut!

Yom Kippur and Anavah

Rosh Hashanah is, of course, followed by Yom Kippur, the Day of Atonement. One would expect the tone of Rosh Hashanah to be quite serious. After all, we are being judged and our futures are at stake. Nevertheless, the day is celebrated — food and drink, fine clothes, cards and greetings. In our communities there is a festive atmosphere as friends and family wish each other the best for the upcoming year.

In stark contrast, Yom Kippur is the day of trembling, a time when "you shall afflict yourself" (Lev. 23:27). Despite our sins and the consequences of our actions, we manage to hold our heads up. However, after some serious teshuvah (repentance) — with concentrated introspection and honesty — we should be in a different mindset on Yom Kippur. As we beg for atonement and forgiveness we are not proud, happy, or haughty. Rather, we are quite low and *humbled*. If we know what is good for us, we bow our heads, cry in shame, and display as much anivut (humility) as we can muster. As we proclaim at the conclusion of our prayers on Yom Kippur during the *Avinu Malkeinu* ("Our Father, Our King") prayer in Ne'ilah, "Our Father, Our King, be gracious with us and answer us though we have no worthy deeds; treat us with charity and kindness and save us." Our only hope for salvation comes when we strip away all egos and realize that it is God's kindness and grace that sustains us, not any of our own actions.

Succot and Yirat Chet

The remaining section of the holiday text in Leviticus 23 actually is a bit puzzling. From verses 33–37, the Torah relates the dates and holiness of the festivals of Succot and Shemini

Atzeret. Verses 37 and 38 summarize the unified concept of the holidays (with language that echoes that of verses 2 and 4) and then verses 39–43 describe the holiday of Succot again, only this time with much greater detail, including the mitzvot of the four species and the succah itself. All of this could most certainly have been integrated into one section. Unless, of course, there are other lessons, perhaps ethical lessons, being taught with these days, as well!

The first time Succot is described here, in verses 33–36, the Torah tells us almost nothing. The bare-bone description is that on the fifteenth of the month a seven day holiday begins, and on the first and seventh day work is prohibited. There is no why or wherefore! One can assume that as we descend from the intensity of Yom Kippur we are shell-shocked. We sinned in the past and we have repented. We hope that our prayers have been accepted and that we will be in for a good year. We are also likely afraid of our own shadows in a spiritual sense. We are afraid to resume regular life; we may fall back into familiar patterns of sin. We might well retreat from spirituality rather than build on it. Forget about any of the rituals or obligations; what Succot represents is an island where we can regain equilibrium. We can fear sin and live spiritually, but at the same time not be paralyzed by it. This is not about actions and conduct; it is about balancing yirat chet with living.

Shemini Atzeret and Kedushah

In verse 35 the Torah slips in a reference to another holiday — Shemini Atzeret. The verse states: "... on the eighth day there shall be a holy convocation for you and you shall offer a fire offering to God, it is an assembly (*atzeret*), you shall not do any work." Effectively, God tells us nothing about this day other than calling it *atzeret*. It has no rituals, no special prayers, and it is not linked to any historical event. So what is it?

Rashi explains that God is saying, "I want you to pause or stop with me (*atzarti etchem etzli*)." He then relates an analogy: "It is like a king who invited his sons to a party for a predetermined time. When the time came for all to leave, the king said to his sons, 'My sons, I request that you stay with me just one more day. Your parting from me is difficult.'" After the experience of the Yamim Nora'im and the spiritual balancing of Succot, we are *kadosh*, we are holy. God recognizes what we have achieved, that we are truly worthy of identification as His children. It is as if there is a magnetic attraction between His holiness and spirit and ours. Shemini Atzeret reflects our ability to acquire and sustain kedushah.

Ruach HaKodesh and Techiyat Hameitim

This should be our stopping point. We have completed our circuit of the holidays *and* we have discussed each of the character traits that Ramchal detailed in *Mesilat Yesharim*. It is rather impressive how they actually match. However, R' Pinchas ben Yair left us with two remaining levels: ruach hakodesh (holy spirituality) and techiyat hameitim (resurrection). Even though we seem to have run out of time and dates, could the Torah portion of the holidays have accounted for these as well?

As mentioned above, just when we thought we were finished with the holidays and the lessons, even to the point of providing a summary statement (verses 37 and 38), the Torah started up again by revisiting Succot. This time, however, the holiday gets a more involved and detailed treatment. The verses set out the basic requirements for the *arba minim*, the four species — the *lulav* (palm branch), *etrog* (citron), *hadasim* (myrtle branches), and *aravot* (willow branches) — as well as the requirements and reasons for the succah itself. Other than the detailed description of the Omer, the verses for the other holidays did not provide the details of the main ritual observances. So, the question arises: what is special about Succot or these mitzvot?

The characteristic of ruach hakodesh, holy spirituality, goes beyond what our senses experience, what the physical world and logic tell us. This is a higher plane, *l'maalah min hateva* (above nature, or supernatural). Yes, there are quite a number of explanations regarding the mitzvah of the four species. However, I must confess that I still do not have the slightest clue about what God wants us to accomplish as we carry and wave these fruits and leaves. Why these species? Why wave them? Why on Succot? Judaism is, for the most part, a very rational and orderly religion. Yet, when we march around with the lulav and etrog there is a part of me that thinks that this must look quite silly! It seems almost pagan and superstitious. Fundamentally, what is God asking of us, and what is He getting out of this?

While I have a better understanding of the symbolism of the succah, this too feels quite foreign. We leave our homes and eat and sleep in a hut with plant matter as a roof. Not only that, but each night we invite the spiritual giants of our past, Avraham, Yitzchak, Yaacov, Yosef, Moshe, Aharon, and David, to visit with us.

While I do not understand all that is going on, what I can see is that these are extremely spiritual actions. We are performing acts that make little or no sense on our plane of existence, but that have obvious and important impact in the spiritual realms. This is the essence of ruach hakodesh — accomplishing and experiencing on levels beyond our own comprehension. The Torah sets these mitzvot apart, as if they are a part of our physical reality, are so much holier and spiritual than they seem — which in turn means we have the potential to be so much holier and more spiritual than we think we are!

Finally, we reach the last and highest level. This is the level beyond the experience of the world as we know it now. Every other characteristic has been a part of Jewish life and heritage. There are great men who have achieved every other level. Techiyat hameitim, resurrection, is associated with the time of Mashiach, an event that we cannot reasonably understand or explain. I approach this with more than a little fear. I feel that I am out of my depth, that I may not fully comprehend. The only way I can move forward here is to anchor myself to the simple words of the text.

If we flip back to Succot I, described in verses 33–36, we find that the Torah establishes the seven day holiday of Succot (34), sets the first day apart as a holy convocation (35), and then there is an eighth day, called an assembly (atzeret) on which offerings are brought and no work is performed (36). The text regarding the eighth day is clearly set apart from the holiness of the first day (it is in a separate verse) and it is not linked grammatically with a *vav* (the connecting letter, often translated as "and") to the seven days mentioned in the verse. In other words, it is an eighth day in relation to the seven of Succot, but it is a separate entity, a separate holiness or spirit from Succot. Stated another way, Succot passes on and something new takes its place.

However, in the verses of Succot II, 39–43, the description of this eighth day and its relationship to Succot is quite different. Verse 39 states: "But on the fifteenth day of the seventh month, when you gather in the crop of the land, you shall celebrate God's festival for a seven day period; the first day is a rest day and the eighth day is a rest day." The verse seems to make no sense: we celebrate for *seven* days… the first *and* the *eighth* days are rest days. Is the holiday seven days or eight days? Are they part of one celebration, or are they two separate holidays? Finally, where did the concept of assembly (atzeret) on the eighth go?

I very humbly suggest that this ambiguous eighth day is the embodiment of *techiyat hameitim.* It is here but it's not. Succot seems finished, but now it is not! This eighth day in Succot II is not our Shemini Atzeret. It is not called an atzeret; it is just *yom hashemini*, the eighth day. In the time of Mashiach God will never say, "Your parting from Me is difficult," since we will always be in His presence. That day will simply be the eighth day of Succot, a day that was associated with the highest level of celebration for the dedication of the Holy Temple, the *Beit Hamikdash* in the times of King Shlomo.

It goes without saying that we could all benefit from studying Ramchal's words in *Mesilat Yesharim* and internalizing them. If we do this, our lives will certainly be richer and we will grow closer to God. But perhaps if we integrate his lessons and approach together with a full appreciation and understanding of each of our annual holidays, our mo'adei hashanah, we will be able to reach levels even higher than he targeted. The directions are certainly in our hands.

• • • Fish Out of Water • • •

Many of the thoughts and ideas in this book are not particularly deep or complex. Rather, they are reflections on the ordinary — the days and events that we encounter over and over again. We pass them so regularly and automatically that we bury their meaning and significance. We concentrate so much on the "hows," the legal details of the performance, that we often do not reflect on the "why." This is most true in connection with rituals that are weekly and daily. When was the last time you thought about the meaning of that blessing you make when you eat a snack? Why is the Psalm for each day different? Why do we read the Torah on certain days of the week (regular, non-holiday weeks) and not on others? This last question intrigues me most of all because it leads to a connection that illuminates the character of each of our weekdays.

Exodus 15:22 is the very first verse after the Torah's description of the crossing of the Red Sea. It states:

> Moshe caused Israel to journey from the Red Sea
> and they went out to the wilderness of Shur; and
> they journeyed for three days in the wilderness but
> they did not find water.

They then arrive at a place called Mara, where there is water, but the water is bitter and not drinkable. The people panic and complain to Moshe that they need water. Moshe prays to God who then throws a tree into the bitter waters, sweetening them. In the same verse that describes how God sweetened the water, we read: "There He established for the nation a decree and an ordinance and there He tested it" (Ex. 15:26).

As you read this narrative, you get a feeling that the pieces do not add up to the whole story. First, why does the text emphasize three days without water? When dealing with millions of people, even a few hours without water would be enough to start a panic. Why does God not simply give them water (as in water from the rock, as He does later)? It seems rather elaborate to bring them to the bitter water, then to sweeten it with the wood. Finally, what does any of this have to do with decrees and ordinances?

The Talmud interprets this incident in a very non-literal way and in fact establishes that this is the source for an important religious practice. Those that interpret the text say that the only 'water' is actually Torah; since they traveled three days [from the miracles at the Red Sea] without Torah, they became depressed. Accordingly, the prophets among them stood and established that they should [publicly] read the Torah on Shabbat, Monday, and Thursday so that they would not tarry three days without Torah (*Bava Kama* 82a).

In other words, this story is not about the physical needs of the Jews. It speaks to their spiritual longing. After they witnessed the miracles of the sea, once they reached great heights in belief in God, they longed for — thirsted for — Torah. They did not want to wait six more weeks until Sinai. After just three days, they demanded Torah. Rashi tells us, quoting the Talmud in *Sanhedrin* 40, that God gave to them parts of the Torah at Mara — the laws of Shabbat, the laws of the Red Heifer, and the laws of court procedure.

While there is much to learn from the language of the text and while this explanation raises many questions of its own, let us stay focused on the first Talmudic text that we quoted.

The fact that the Jews could not go three days without Torah led *someone* to establish the practice of publicly reading from the Torah on Monday, Thursday, and Shabbat. That someone was either Moshe himself, as the Rambam states (*Hilchot Tefila* 12:1), or the prophets who led at the time the Jews were first exiled to Babylon, as the Torah Temima argues. Regardless of when this practice was established, it is now well ingrained. So that we do not go more than three days without reading the Torah, in addition to the Shabbat, we read it publicly on Monday and Thursday.

But why these days and not another set of days? One explanation is based on a Midrash that explains that when Moshe ascended to receive the second Tablets, he went up on a Thursday and descended on a Monday. However, this explanation does not fit if we accept that this custom was established at Mara, months before Moshe received the second Tablets.

To discover the answer, I believe that we have to once again go back to the beginning, to the six days of creation. Aspects of the character of each day are fixed in God's actions on that day. When we define the character of Monday (the second day) and Thursday (the fifth day) we will see that they directly relate to the Mara story.

The six days of creation can be summarized as follows:

Day One — Heaven and earth and *light* (Gen. 1:1–5)

Day Two — Separation of the upper and lower *water* (Gen. 1:6–8)

Day Three — Dry *land*, vegetation sprouting from the *land* (Gen. 1:9–13)

Day Four — Sun, moon, stars = *light* (Gen. 1:14–19)

Day Five — The living creatures from the *water* (Gen. 1:20–23)

Day Six — The living creatures from the *land* (including man) (Gen. 1:24–31)

As you can see from this representation, the Six Days of Creation are actually two cycles of three days each. The creation of Days One, Two, and Three are repeated on Days Four, Five, and Six, respectively. Day Two and Day Five are both the days of *water*. The analogy that the Torah establishes for its importance to the Jewish People is *water*. It thus makes sense that if Moshe, or even later sages, wanted to reinforce this message and analogy, they would establish Torah reading on the days of *water*. This may well solve the mystery.

• • • TIME AND PLACE • • •

While writing this book about Jewish time, my personal life was consumed by Jewish place — my family and I made *aliyah* to our holy Land of Israel. The days on the Jewish calendar have so much more meaning here. There is the vibrancy of collective experience, to be celebrating as a Jew in the Jewish homeland. There is a living connection to history, being at or near where the events occurred. (We, in fact, actually live on the same ground as the Chashmona'im). Perhaps most important, there is a holiness that resonates, which elevates every nuance of observance. I feel that every word in this book has been influenced by this holiness.

Israel is a place of connection. In our short time here I have encountered buddies from elementary school and summer camp days, friends from yeshivot that I attended, former co-workers and neighbors, and even long-lost relatives. I am thus regularly revisiting the times and memories of my life within my own lifetime. I believe that this is how God wants us to live His time. He wants us constantly to experience leaving Egypt, receiving the Torah, and living in the desert. We are modern day Maccabees, we can turn fast days into festivals, and we can systematically manage our spiritual growth and development in synch with the seasons. In Deuteronomy 4:4, Moshe proclaims: "But you who connect to the Lord, your God — you are all alive *today*." If we connect His dates and follow the lines we can achieve completion.